Ten Traits of Resilience

Other titles from Bloomsbury Education

Leading from the Edge by James Hilton

Creating Tomorrow's Schools Today by Richard Gerver

Mark. Plan. Teach. by Ross Morrison McGill

Narrowing the Attainment Gap by Daniel Sobel

How to Survive in Teaching by Dr Emma Kell

Live Well, Teach Well by Abigail Mann

Ten Traits of Resilience

Achieving positivity and purpose in school leadership

by James Hilton

Foreword by Dr Andy Cope

BLOOMSBURY EDUCATION
LONDON OXFORD NEW YORK NEW DELHI SYDNEY

BLOOMSBURY EDUCATION
Bloomsbury Publishing Plc
50 Bedford Square, London, WC1B 3DP, UK

BLOOMSBURY, BLOOMSBURY EDUCATION and the Diana logo are trademarks of Bloomsbury Publishing Plc

First published in Great Britain 2018

A catalogue record for this book is available from the British Library.

ISBN: PB: 978-1-4729-5150-2; ePDF: 978-1-4729-5151-9; ePub: 978-1-4729-5152-6

2 4 6 8 10 9 7 5 3 1 (paperback)

Typeset by Newgen KnowledgeWorks Pvt. Ltd., Chennai, India
Printed and bound by CPI Group (UK) Ltd, Croydon CR0 4YY

Contents

Acknowledgements

This book would not have been possible without the kindness, generosity and wisdom of the following people:

Dr Andy Cope, Richard Gerver, Martyn Reah, Wendy Rose, and Jann and Tony Tucker.

I would also like to thank the following people for allowing me to include their thoughts and words within the book:

Sharon de Caestecker, Elain Crewe, Viv Grant, Kim Johnson, Ross Morrison McGill, Patrick Ottley-O'Connor and Ayesha Weston.

Foreword

I trained to be a teacher way back in 1993 BC (Before Computers). No Google. No interactive whiteboards. No emails. No tablets. Best of all, no Ofsted or lesson observations.

My subject was 'business and economics' and my mentor was the thoroughly Welsh Mr Jones. I assumed he'd been assigned mentoring duties because he had the right skill set. You know, all that special 'soft' stuff, like motivating, listening, caring and giving a shit.

It turned out that Mr Jones was 'special', just not in the way I imagined. There was chalk dust everywhere. It's odd, but when Mr Jones returned from the gents, he always seemed to have some under his nose.

For the first couple of weeks I was assigned to sit and watch the master craftsman weave his magic. Mr Jones seemed to have made being disorganised an art form. He had an air of not caring which class was coming through the door. He'd ask them – 'Which age group are you? Can you remember what we covered last time?' There was an awful lot of 'Turn to page 23 and copy it out'.

While the teenagers were copying things from their textbook, it gave me a lot of time to look around. There were wall displays from the '80s and a coffee cup on the windowsill with mould floating in it. My mentor had a name card on his desk – one of those that you get when you go on a course, which is basically a folded-over piece of cardboard. On one side he'd written 'Taffy Jones' (which would nowadays be considered a mildly racist self-insult) and on the other 'DILLIGAF'. I wondered what DILLIGAF meant. I assumed it was Welsh. His home town perhaps? Remember, this was pre-Google.

One day, after I'd sat through a particularly inadequate lesson, Jonesy and I went for a pint. I dared to ask him how he thought the lesson had gone and he just shrugged and supped. 'DILLIGAF,' he belched.

'DILLIGAF?' I asked, eyebrows raised.

Jonesy was supping again. This time he wiped away the froth with his sleeve and explained, 'Do I look like I give a f***?'

Jonesy was ace. I learned so much, not least that I didn't actually want to be a teacher. I've subsequently also learned that people like Jonesy have been weeded out of the profession. As the rough and tumble has become rougher and more tumbly, they've been found out. *Phew!*

So who's left? If the DILLIGAFs have gone, I guess it's the TWGASFs ('those who give a serious f***') who remain. This book is for all you TWGASFs out there.

Before I pass you over to James, let me explain the paradox within (or it might be an oxymoron, I've never quite grasped the difference). The bad news is that the more you care about making a difference, the higher your chances of exhaustion and burnout. And yet the good news mirrors it – the more you care about making a difference, the higher your chances of surviving and thriving.

Dostoevsky says the same thing, more poetically: 'Pain and suffering are always inevitable for a large intelligence and a deep heart.' What he means is those who care the most are more likely to suffer the most. The ones who can't be bothered have inoculated themselves against real stress. If you don't give a monkey's about work, the kids or your colleagues, you will survive the rough and tumble just fine. But your lack of caring also means you're missing out on the really good stuff – passion, energy, purpose, drive, vigour – all the things that tally with that precious gift of being alive.

Hywel Roberts talks about what he calls 'botheredness' and, like most things, I think it comes on a spectrum. As you're about to find out, James has a very interesting backstory that suggests you can perhaps care too much, a sort of 'extreme botheredness' that ends up making you poorly. The best teachers, doctors, nurses, police and school leaders suffer from this. If they can't do their job properly, it pains them. Their passion flares up and their botheredness destroys them, like a microwaved jacket potato, from the inside out.

So, although it's true that you can be *too bothered,* I'd argue (as does James) that it's a much better place than the apathetic 'DILLIGAF' end of the spectrum.

You'll love this book. Not just because it's loveable, but also because you and the author have so much in common. He cares too. Like crazy. In fact, James's botheredness nearly killed him.

But that was then. James has come out the other end better, stronger, more emotionally resilient and a whole lot wiser. So please don't stop caring. Not ever. James will show you how to channel your passion and bounce back when the inevitable happens. This book is crammed with wisdom. I'm pretty sure James has written it for the 25-year-old version of himself.

Enjoy.

Dr Andy Cope

Andy is the UK's first, only and therefore foremost Dr of Happiness. He delivers positive psychology programmes all over the world and is lucky enough to work with school leaders, teachers and children on a regular basis. Andy has crafted a 'GCSE wellbeing' syllabus that he hopes, one day, will make it onto the school curriculum. Wouldn't it be great to see happiness, wellbeing and resilience alongside maths, science and English?

Introduction

Hello and thank you for making it this far into my book! If you have already purchased this copy then thank you. If you are browsing the shelf, go on, buy it, you know you want to!

My name is James and I spent 26 years in primary education (which is more than you get for murder these days). 23 of those years were spent in senior leadership positions in the Midlands. I was a deputy head of a large primary school for eight years and a headteacher for 15 years. Latterly, I was head of one of the largest primary schools in Britain, a job that I loved but found very challenging, and in 2006 to 2007 I had a nervous breakdown brought on by work-related stress. After a six-month period of absence and a course of cognitive behaviour therapy I returned to work, more self-aware than before and armed with a toolbox of coping strategies. This story I told in my book, *Leading from the Edge*.

These days, I make my living as an author and speaker concentrating on leadership and wellbeing. Being one step removed from a school leadership role, I can reflect openly and honestly on some of the things that I got right and wrong, in a way that would have been difficult to do when still in post. In doing so I hope that my reflections will give other school leaders strength, as well as helping them to avoid some of the pitfalls of leadership that I fell into over the years.

As my career has developed, I have become very interested in understanding what makes resilient schools. We are living in a world of exponential change. The teaching profession bears little relationship to the one that I joined as an enthusiastic but wet-behind-the-ears young teacher 30 years ago. In my first year of teaching I recall that we had no school uniform, no formalised curriculum, no standardised national testing and very little in the way of accountability. We had one parents' evening a year and I do not even recall writing children's reports. We had one staff meeting a week and at lunchtime we would all disappear to the staffroom. You knew which room was the staffroom not because it had a sign on it (that had fallen off a long time ago) but because it had a fog of cigarette smoke billowing from under the door. We would stay in there for a whole hour apart from on a Friday, when the entire teaching staff, including the headteacher, would go to the local pub, leaving the pupils in the care of the midday supervisors, or 'dinner ladies' as they were known back then. Having consumed two pints of beer or two glasses of wine, depending on taste, we would then return to 'teach' the afternoon session, which usually consisted of 'NMAs' or non-marking activities as they were known. I do remember there being a very nice Polish cook in the kitchens who always insisted on giving me double portions of chips at lunchtime because she thought I needed fattening up. I don't think that she saw instant results from the project, but 30 years on she would probably be quite pleased with the outcome!

Now I am not suggesting that these were in some ways the 'good old days'. They were not. There was very little in the way of quality assurance of teaching (I only remember being observed once in my first year), and children who fell behind tended to stay behind. For many of you reading this the world I describe will seem quite alien. The reality is that the education system is changing faster than at any point that I can ever recall. Even 20 years ago the notion of state-funded schools opting out of local authority control would have seemed improbable. My point is this: it is almost impossible to predict what the next ten years may bring in terms of education reform, let alone imagine what schools will look like in 20 or even 30 years' time. One thing I do know is that to survive and thrive schools will need to be resilient places.

At the time that I am writing, there is a welcome emphasis on mental health in schools. Much of it centres on the mental wellbeing of students. This is, of course, hugely important; however, there will be little accomplished in this area unless we consider the resilience of teachers who are having to react and adapt to a tidal wave of change. Resilience is becoming a hot topic in schools. It is in many ways the antithesis of teacher burnout, a phenomenon that sees many teachers leave the profession within five years of qualification and many school leaders retire early. Ten years ago, wellbeing was not something on the agenda for many schools and some school leaders would have seen it as something 'woolly' and 'touchy-feely'. Thankfully, attitudes are changing, and senior leadership teams who ignore the issue of wellbeing are, frankly, missing a trick. Staff absence and difficulties in recruiting and retaining teachers remains one of the biggest barriers to school improvement and the education system that our children need and deserve. Teaching is one of the best jobs in the world. However, it is a job full of highs and lows: at times incredibly rewarding; at others very stressful. The further you go up the leadership ladder, the more amplified these highs and lows may seem. School leadership is a privilege. The opportunity to shape the vision for the future of our children is one of the most important and influential jobs in the world.

The issue of teacher resilience from a school leadership point of view is therefore what I want to concentrate on in this book. After my own resilience failed spectacularly ten years ago, I am fascinated as to why some individuals stay resilient in life whilst others do not. I do not claim to be an academic; I swore when I finished university that I would never take another exam and I never have. So, if you are after a textbook study, this really is not the book for you and I don't mind if you put it back on the shelf. (I'm not looking!)

If you are still with me then, in this book, I want to explore with you the nature of personal resilience, because it is only by understanding the nature of individual resilience that we can, as school leaders, hope to grow our own resilience *and* build a resilient school that can survive and thrive in a world of exponential change.

Time to reflect

So, what does resilience mean to you?

1 If you are feeling artistic, draw an image of what you see when you think of resilience.

2 If you are more of a words person, write down the words you associate with resilience instead.

Resilience is the virtue that enables people to move through hardship and become better. No one escapes pain, fear, and suffering. Yet from pain can come wisdom, from fear can come courage, from suffering can come strength – if we have the virtue of resilience.

Eric Greitens (2015)

'Resilience' is often defined as springing back to an original shape after having been bent or stretched, or readily recovering from shock. 'Bouncebackability' is a more user-friendly phrase sometimes used to describe the phenomenon. Dr Al Siebert takes this further and describes resilience as being like a rubber band. As with people, rubber bands come in different shapes and sizes but are designed to be stretched. However, if the rubber band is overstretched for significant periods of time or placed in a very hot environment, the integrity of the rubber starts to break down. Stretch the rubber band too far altogether and you run the risk of the band snapping (Siebert 2005).

A couple of things strike me here.

Firstly, whilst we all reach a point in our lives when we stop growing in height (I am at the stage where I am now growing outwards!), we never stop growing, changing and adapting both mentally and emotionally. As such, it is unlikely that we ever 'snap back' from life's events exactly as we were before. We learn, we grow, we adapt.

Also, there is not just one kind of resilience. I am immensely lucky to be writing this book in a cottage on the Welsh coast overlooking the Irish Sea. From the window I can see a tree, a tall oak I think, that given its distorted shape was clearly struck by lightning some years ago. Now, having been in a house that was struck by lightning when I was 14 years old, I can assure you that this is, indeed, a life-changing event. The tree and I have both adapted and got over the event and continue to grow, albeit in a slightly different way. But also from my window I can see clearly, as in many places along the Welsh coast, a line of trees whose branches and leaves grow to the east side of the tree – in other words away from the shoreline. These are not trees that have necessarily experienced some kind of cataclysmic event, but they have learned to thrive under the near constant pressure of the winds that blow inland from the sea.

For me, this analogy represents the two kinds of resilience that staff in schools, and senior leaders in particular, need to possess.

On the one hand, we need the ability to be able to recover and adapt from the 'curveballs' that will inevitably be thrown our way from time to time. Some years ago, whilst staying in this cottage, I walked with family and friends on the coastal path from Penbryn to Llangrannog in Ceredigion. It looked a straightforward walk in the guidebook, but the reality was that there were huge gullies and steep climbs along the way. These would have been more obvious if we had looked at the contour lines on an Ordnance Survey map (something that I learned to do in A-level geography, which is now, doubtless, an expectation of Foundation Stage children!). School leadership comes with no OS map. We have a sense of the direction we wish to travel, but can rarely anticipate the gullies and steep climbs along the way.

On the other hand, resilience in schools is about recognising that change is like the wind blowing in off the sea. There will be times of calm, but these will never be as long as we might reasonably hope and we need to be realistic about this and able to continue to grow, not because of those winds of change necessarily but sometimes in spite of them.

Not an heroic superhuman quality, but 'ordinary magic': teach, and teach well over time, requires everyday resilience.

Christopher Day and Quing Gu (2014)

Time to reflect

- What has been the biggest single event or action that has knocked you off course in your career? (If you haven't got one, consider yourself blessed!)

- Why was it so significant?

- What did you learn from it?

- What three things represent the winds of change that you continue to grow professionally in spite of?

  1

  2

  3

- How do you minimise their effect and ameliorate them?

There is little doubt in my mind that our resilience levels are different from person to person and partly depend on our experiences, which shape our outlook and approach to life.

David is a close friend of mine; we taught together some years ago. He is an effervescent and dynamic character and is, without doubt, one of the most resilient people I have ever worked with. I met him recently for a pint (well, two or three if I am being honest!). Having exhausted the usual topics of TV and film, we got on to talking about various projects we were currently involved in and I told him that I was writing a book on resilience. I asked him what was the secret of his resilience, and he told me a story that I had never heard before.

When David was eight, his father, in a fit of rage, picked him up under his arms and hurled him across the lounge. He did so with such force that he hit the closed door into the hall, breaking the door frame and leaving David bruised, winded and distraught. Not surprisingly, this incident has stayed with him his whole life.

'When you have been through something like that, at the hands of your own father, nothing seems as bad, and when I encounter hard times, I remind myself of that,' he told me.

David's story reminded me of a conversation I had with a teacher at a conference where I had been speaking a few weeks earlier. The teacher in question gave up part of her weekends and holidays working as a counsellor with ex-service personnel who had experienced life-changing injuries. She told me of the soldier that she was currently working with who had lost an arm and two legs in a roadside explosion in the war in Iraq. She described him as an amazing man and one of the most resilient people she had ever met. She too asked him what his secret was and he replied that having experienced such a traumatic and life-changing event, he had little left to fear in life.

Our experiences in life tend to shape our resilience, but the good news is that we do not need to be a slave to those experiences, and it is possible to learn to build up resilience proactively.

I want you to do something for me. You're going to have to trust me here, okay?

I want you to picture yourself travelling in a hot air balloon. Now, I am going to have to confess to you that I have never been in one and, as you have to ply me with alcohol before I will even get on board an aeroplane, it is not terribly likely that I will be floating in a balloon above your house any time soon! So I am not claiming to be an expert in the science of balloon travel. Nonetheless, I have always harboured a romantic notion of travelling peacefully in this manner. It seems to me that school leadership is a little like travelling in a balloon. We start with the deep-rooted, hopeful expectation that our journey will be exhilarating but essentially smooth! However, there is an optimum height at which to travel. Travel too high and you run the risk of drifting into the clouds, losing clear vision and your touch with reality. Travel too low and you are at risk from any number of hazards: tall trees, telegraph poles, church spires to name but a few! It is finding the balance that is the key to successful school leadership.

I am what you might term a cautious optimist. I try to look for the best in situations and the best in other people, but I do like the idea of a safety net. For example, if I am giving a presentation at a conference I will not only save my slides on my laptop but I will also keep a backup on a memory stick and also in an online Dropbox account. I don't like having all my eggs in one basket and similarly this is my concern about my fantasy of hot air balloon travel. I am concerned that the wicker basket that I am standing in is suspended from just the one balloon! What if the fabric tears? Well, I think I am probably scuppered. And I think resilience is a little bit like that. Relying on just one thing to keep us afloat seems a pretty risky strategy to me.

I much prefer the idea of my wicker basket being held aloft by a number of balloons. In this way, if one of the balloons deflates, I have sufficient other resources to be able to continue on my way.

I want to stretch my analogy of the hot air balloons a little further. I believe that in order to understand why some people remain resilient and others do not, it is important to identify aspects of the behaviour of people who stay resilient over time. These are the traits of resilience, if you will. I am going to suggest that there are ten of these traits that characterise both resilient people and resilient schools: a sense of purpose, optimism, trust, courage, decisiveness, asking for help, a sense of fun, curiosity, taking care of yourself and others, and turning adversity into opportunity. Think of each of these traits as an individual balloon attached to the basket in which you are travelling. I am sure that there will be somebody out there who will tell me that this is not scientifically possible, and this may well be the case. However, travelling aloft suspended by ten balloons seems a much safer option to me than being carried purely by one.

In this book we will explore each of these balloons, or traits, in turn, looking at how they are reflected in resilient people and the lessons that we can take from them for school leadership. One thing I will say from the outset is that it is unreasonable, as school leaders, to expect yourself to keep all these balloons fully inflated at all times. For example, one of the traits people and schools aspire to is the ability to remain optimistic. Know this: living in the real world, you can't expect yourself to be optimistic 100 per cent of the time. Don't beat yourself up about it. That is not allowed. You are human after all and it is actually okay *not* to feel okay all of the time!

The key though, to resilience, both as an individual and as a school, is to keep the majority of those ten balloons inflated at any one time and to ensure that you don't leave any one balloon deflated for long periods.

A plea here, as you read this book: please engage with the exercises and take notes. Take your time in considering your answers to the reflective questions and write them either in the spaces within the boxes or on a separate piece of paper. The act of doing so will help to increase self-awareness, which, in turn, helps build resilience.

So, without further ado let's climb into the wicker basket of school leadership and take a ride!

1 A sense of purpose

Efforts and courage are not enough without purpose and direction.

John F. Kennedy

I would imagine if you are reading this book you are perhaps either a senior leader in a school or aspire to be one in the near future. Either way, you are very welcome! Like all teachers, you will be living a life at a hectic pace, where you arrive at school in the morning with a plan for the day, only to find five minutes later that you have to reformulate that plan in light of changing circumstances, such as the absence of a colleague, a burst water pipe in the girls' toilets, or a stray dog running around the playground just as the children are about to arrive. The list is endless and as such it leaves us with few opportunities to reflect. I am not talking so much about the self-evaluation of lessons or our teaching style; we do that all the time and we are usually pretty hard on ourselves. No, rather I am talking about self-awareness, and understanding the way that we think and sometimes behave.

In this chapter, we are going to examine the first of the ten balloons of resilience that help to keep us as school leaders, and schools as a whole, aloft and on our way. That balloon is a sense of purpose.

A personal sense of purpose

All animals, including us humans, have a sense of purpose deeply hardwired into our primitive or reptilian (as it is sometimes known) brain. That purpose is to survive; it is our fight or flight response. What sets humans apart from other animals is that we are capable of rational, sophisticated thinking and the ability to make clear choices for ourselves. We crave a sense of direction and purpose that is influenced by our decision making.

Purpose is a necessary component of a happy and fulfilling life.

> *By focusing our attention externally, and giving us a constant source of activity to channel our mental energies into, purpose means that we spend less immersed in the associational chatter of our minds – the chatter which often triggers negative thoughts and feelings.*
>
> Steve Taylor (2013)

Taylor argues that a sense of purpose can enhance our self-esteem. If we feel that we are overcoming challenges and moving closer to our goals, our confidence levels rise, enhancing our abilities to deal with further challenges. As the saying goes, 'success breeds success'.

A sense of purpose is closely linked with a sense of hope. Working towards goals that we help to determine implies that we feel that those goals are attainable, and that our life, or the lives of others that we seek to help, will change for the better once we achieve them.

Time to reflect

- Do you remember a specific point in your life when you decided that you wanted to teach?

- If so, when was that?

- What was it that drew you to teaching as a profession?

Now, I'm going to make something of a confession. It is something that as a professional I always found rather embarrassing. It is nothing physical (although I do have webbed toes on my right foot, which does make me a strong swimmer but I only go round in circles!), but it is something that I felt troubled by, particularly in the early part of my career.

You see I never wanted to become a teacher. I have met many wonderful teachers over the years who seemed to have experienced some kind of calling, often from an early age. My own daughter, Julia, who is now in her fourth year of teaching, played schools with her dolls and her teddy bears from an early age. Arguably, she may have been influenced by the fact that both of her parents were teachers, but I believe it was more than that. She had a gift with younger children and on family holidays abroad she would acquire a growing band of followers around the poolside as the week progressed, much to the consternation of their parents who had paid good money for their offspring to attend 'kids' clubs', which became largely redundant with Julia around.

My story was quite different. There was no 'great calling'. Nor was there a 'blinding light' moment when my future path became clear.

I had enjoyed drama and taking part in school plays from a young age. When I was in sixth form, I was directed by my English teacher in a production of *The Wizard of Oz*. I played the part of the Tin Man and (notwithstanding the incident when some smart alec substituted real oil for water in the oil can I was supposed to gargle from), I loved every minute of it and was determined to apply for university drama courses. My English teacher, who was one of the very few staff members I felt truly believed in me, gently suggested that, as a drama degree was widely dismissed as preparation for a career in acting in those days and was perceived as having limited application to the wider world of work, I should apply to study a degree in drama and education and in that way I would have two strings to my bow.

I loved the course, particularly those periods preparing for and performing plays. Many people studying had aspirations to work in television, but as the years went by I realised many students in the year groups above me did not realise their aspirations. Of those that did, Nick Hancock went on to become the presenter of the long-running sports quiz *They Think It's All Over* on the BBC. Another surfaced some years later as a designer on the BBC makeover show *Changing Rooms*.

A third, allegedly, sung on the original cast recording of *Evita* (which, if true, was pretty impressive) and a fourth became a topless model (which was rather less impressive). It seemed my route to stardom was rather less than guaranteed and so I drifted towards teaching, which I had enjoyed more and more as the course had progressed. It would, at least, pretty much guarantee me an income.

So there it is, the secret is out. I went into teaching for practical reasons rather than any great calling, but here is another thing: I really was not very good at it at first. I worked hard enough and I liked the children in my first class, many of whose names I still remember to this day (particularly Catherine, who always had seconds at lunch when she really didn't need it and one day threw up copious quantities of sponge and pink custard over me), but there was just no passion in my teaching. There was no real sense of purpose to what I was doing. Yes, I worked hard and with some skill, but in truth I was mediocre at best.

It was not until my second year of teaching that things started to change. But that was not down to one event but to two nine-year-old children.

Richard was a book lover. He hated PE and was not particularly popular with the other children. He would be in the medical room at playtimes whenever he could invent a reason or asking for jobs at playtime, which his previous class teacher had found as something of an irritant. When he did go outside at break, you would usually find him in a corner of the playground with his head buried in a book, usually Roald Dahl.

We developed a connection over the year – I was no great lover of sport either, despite inheriting the mantle of manager of the school football team. I encouraged Richard to join the school newspaper and he came along as a 'journalist' and reported on all our fixtures. It played to his skills and as the team players quite enjoyed being glorified in print, he grew in popularity.

At parents' evening at the end of the year, his parents gratefully gave me a hardback copy of *Matilda*, which of course partly tells the story of a misunderstood child who finds a teacher who understands and believes in her. The book was simply inscribed 'With grateful thanks' inside the front cover and signed by his parents, but most meaningfully, by Richard himself. I have the book to this day.

Philip, by contrast, was a popular member of the class but struggled with reading and particularly maths. We were carrying out two parallel projects in the summer term. There was a science project on electricity and circuits, lighting bulbs and turning motors using batteries, leads and switches, and a technology project designing and building motorised buggies using wood, glue, dowelling, wooden wheels and cardboard triangles to reinforce the joints. This technique was often referred to as 'Jinks' method of construction' (I am sure it will be familiar to many of you) and it filled the hearts of cleaners across the land with joy, as they discovered drill holes in the children's desktops. Looking back, there was not that much design involved on the children's part; it was a more of a 'Blue Peter approach' of copy what I do.

Inevitably, some children found the challenges of sawing and drilling wood more challenging than others, but Phillip took to it like a duck to water and finished way ahead of his classmates. So the following week, I trusted him to create something truly of his own design using the techniques he had learned. As he was one of the few who had not nearly sawn his own fingers off, or created a Swiss cheese effect in his desktop, I left him largely to his own devices, returning to him mid-afternoon. He had very skilfully and neatly created a model of a class desk and chair approximately ten centimetres in height. I congratulated him on his efforts and returned to mop up more blood elsewhere in the room.

When we packed away at the end of the afternoon I returned to Philip once more to see the culmination of his efforts. Applying what he had learnt about electric circuits in science, Philip had made a lamp to sit on top of the desk battery taped to the table leg. To the underside of the model chair he had attached a magnet. Whenever the chair (which was now occupied by a plasticine figure of a person) was drawn up to the table, the magnet activated a reed switch under the table top, completing a circuit and switching on the lamp. So, sit at the desk, the light comes on; move the chair away, the light goes off. Genius!

Although these two children had comparatively little to do with one another, they both helped me to realise two things:

- All children have the ability to excel at something and it is often a case of finding what they are good at and tapping into that area of interest to build confidence in other areas.
- I could, and should, strive to make a real difference to children's lives. I like to imagine that Richard is a journalist on a newspaper somewhere and that Philip is a designer for IKEA, but who knows?

I was a little slow to get going, but suddenly I had a real sense of purpose and perhaps I was born to teach after all!

Time to reflect

- When was the last time you felt that you were born to teach?
- What were the circumstances – a particular lesson or event perhaps?
- What were the emotions you experienced at that time?

In the hectic hustle and bustle of school life – with the long days, the meetings, the playground duties, the planning... – it is easy to lose sight of our core purpose, what we are about, and what we set out to achieve.

I may have started out all those years ago on a balloon ride with little sense of direction, almost drifting into teaching and seeing it just as a job. And it is of course that, a job, and one that can take over your whole life if you do not establish clear boundaries, but actually most of us don't just see the payslip at the end of the month; we see something else.

What are the benefits of having a clear personal sense of purpose?

In the long term, having a sense of purpose may actually help us extend our lives! Dan Buettner identified the attributes that most centenarians around the world share, particularly in areas termed 'blue zones', where there was a much higher prevalence of people living beyond 100 (Buettner, 2009). One of these factors was having a strong sense of purpose. A 2009 study of over 70,000 Japanese men and women found that those who had a strong sense of purpose (*ikigai*) tended to live longer than those who didn't (Buettner, 2012).

That purpose may be taking care of grandchildren (or even great grandchildren), or going fishing for food for the family. The nature of the purpose was not as important as the fact that the individuals concerned had a clear purpose for getting out of bed in the morning.

A different study, this time of retired employees of the Shell oil company, concluded that men and women who retired at the age of 55 were more likely to die earlier than those employees who retired at age 65 (Tsai et al., 2005). A further study of almost 17,000 Greeks showed that their risk of death increased by around 50 per cent after retirement (Bamia et al., 2008).

Because of the physical demands of their jobs, the careers of many sportsmen and women finish much earlier than for many in other careers, and many have to 'reinvent themselves'. Some go on to become commentators and TV pundits. Others become involved in charity work or concentrate on developing upcoming talent in their sport. A few sadly seem to lose their way altogether. Football player Paul Gascoigne, often known by his nickname 'Gazza', earned 57 caps playing for England and was widely regarded as one of the best midfielders of his generation. His passion for his job was evident to all: in the 1990 World Cup, he famously cried after receiving a yellow card in the semi-final with West Germany, which would have meant he was suspended for the final itself. Since being sacked as manager of Kettering Town in 2005, he has not worked in football and has had a very public fall from grace, with many unflattering headlines in the press.

For some people, a lack of a clear sense of purpose, or having that sense of purpose removed by a change of circumstances such as redundancy or even retirement, can cause real trauma. Without a clear sense of purpose, we become more susceptible to boredom, anxiety and even depression. (NB: a post-retirement purpose does not include playing golf. As the comedian Jeremy Hardy recently put it, 'When you become interested in golf it's time to book a flight to Switzerland!')

It would seem there may be some risk in finding meaning only in a career! It seems important to revisit and adapt our sense of purpose and find ways to serve that purpose, even after we eventually retire, to improve our prospects of a long and healthy life.

But for the moment, let me ask you this question:

Why do you get up out of your bed each morning and go to work in a school?

I'm sure your answer won't be anything to do with the money or the holidays. It will more likely be the belief that you can make a positive difference in children's lives that gives you direction. Our sense of purpose is partly determined by our values: the things that are most important to us in life, for example, helping others or improving our local community. It is also a reflection of the qualities we respect in others and aspire to ourselves, e.g. respect or generosity. Without values, we can have no sense of direction or moral compass to influence our decision making. We can quite simply lose our way in life.

If you have a strong purpose in life, you don't have to be pushed. Your passion will drive you there.

Roy T. Bennett (2016)

Time to reflect

What three things do you most need in order to be satisfied in your personal life?

1

2

3

What three things do you most need in order to be satisfied in your professional life?

1

2

3

What three qualities do you most admire in other people and aspire to yourself?

1

2

3

However, it is also important to note that a person's values and therefore sense of purpose will inevitably adjust and adapt over time. It would be true to say that my sense of purpose has changed over the years. When I became a school leader, it was not particularly for the increased salary (although with a growing family, I cannot deny that it was an attraction), nor was it for the plaudits or the recognition. Let's face it, if you have a queue at the door, it is unlikely to be made up of parents or members of the press wanting to congratulate you and tell you what a marvellous job you are doing. I suspect that many of us become leaders because we have a view about how children learn best and how staff should be treated in school. We want to influence the direction the balloon should be heading in.

In my second headship, a small traditional village primary that expanded from 150 on roll to over 800 in 12 years, my mission was still to make a positive difference to the lives of children (and staff – you can't do one without the other), but it also became about maintaining a village primary ethos in a rapidly expanding secondary-sized primary school. That was my purpose, and I would often judge the success of some of the decisions we made as a senior leadership team against that criteria.

An evolving sense of purpose

It is perfectly natural that our sense of purpose should evolve and adapt over time, often reacting to events and the cards life deals us. Three years into my second headship, I experienced a nervous breakdown brought on by work-related stress. (This period, my subsequent recovery and return to successful headship, I documented in my first book, *Leading from the Edge*). It is fair to say that this one event, albeit over a period of around 18 months, significantly shifted my outlook and I felt an increasing need to share my story in the hope that it would help other education professionals avoid the traps that I fell into and the crushing sense of isolation that I felt during this time. Thus, my sense of purpose has changed once more.

Time to reflect

Most of us will experience significant experiences or life events (either positive or negative) that shape our outlook and career path. What are the three most significant events for you? What happened? How did they make you feel? What influence did they have on your career path?

1 What happened?

Feelings:

Influence:

2 What happened?

Feelings:

Influence:

3 What happened?

Feelings:

Influence:

Interview skills expert Max Eggert suggests that most interviews start with some variation of the question, 'Tell us a little about yourself' (Eggert, 2007). This is a gift, he argues, because if you prepare well you can take control of the first part of the interview and sell yourself to the panel in the period when they are already rapidly forming opinions of your suitability for the position. He advises that all candidates prepare a short statement that they can memorise, which outlines their experience, suitability and motivation. I advocate this approach as, over the years, it has really helped me to focus in on just what it is James Hilton is actually about and what he stands for. Adopting the same approach and writing a concise statement outlining your sense of purpose in life can really focus the mind.

Time to reflect

In no more than 50 words, write a statement that summarises your sense of purpose in life.

We are by nature purposeful creatures; we just have to find what that purpose is in order to thrive.

> *Your purpose in life is to find your purpose and give your whole heart and soul to it.*
>
> Gautama Buddha

A school-level sense of purpose

A sense of purpose is as important for a thriving school as for any one of the individuals that make up the school population. After all, schools are about human beings, not just brick and mortar (nor exam results and league tables!).

Most people are working towards something in life. Some working in schools will be working towards career advancement. Others may be looking to improve their skills or develop a desired characteristic such as patience, for example. There may be times in our lives when it feels that we are concentrating on getting through a difficult period either personally, e.g. a bereavement, or professionally, e.g. a less favourable Ofsted judgement. Some people, though, can end up trudging through their professional lives feeling undervalued and demotivated but they show up each day. Perhaps their sense of purpose has become focused on one narrow outcome: earning enough money to support themselves and their families. However, this is not sustainable in the long run and such members of staff often become unhappy and demotivated. They tend not to develop their talents beyond what is necessary and therefore do not achieve their full potential. They may do an adequate job but rarely a great one. They end up, as happiness expert and author Dr Andy Cope might put it, as a mediocre version of themselves – much as I did in my first couple of years of teaching. Clearly, this is to the detriment of the education of the children attending school.

There are many potential factors in schools that help staff to stay resilient in what is an intense and pressurised job. These may include recognition of achievements, adequate remuneration for the job, or work–life balance, but also the sense that they are being listened to by the leadership team. In other words, they feel empowered and able to make a contribution to the future direction of the school and 'buy in' to the school sense of purpose, its vision and values.

> *Leaders who refuse to listen will eventually be surrounded by people who have nothing significant to say.*
>
> Andy Stanley (2013)

This is not to say that schools should be run as democracies but nor should they be run as dictatorships either. There is a balance to be struck. Schools need a clear sense of purpose, otherwise staff members may become demotivated. In larger schools, year groups, departments or faculties operate as teams within a larger team; they are wheels within wheels. Without a clear whole-school sense of purpose, how can these smaller teams plan and evaluate their contributions as part of the whole-school direction? Without a clear sense of direction, schools can potentially fragment and chaos ensues.

> *We are purposeful creatures; we need structure, routine and goals to function effectively.*
>
> Rebecca Griffiths (2014)

But surely the purpose of schools is obvious and easy to define, right? It is simply to educate children to allow them to become fully functioning members of society.

At a simplistic level, of course, this is correct. And yet, schools are such interesting and varied places to work and learn in. In my line of employment, I have the privilege of visiting schools across the UK but I am still astounded by the sheer variety in atmosphere and ethos.

I visited a secondary school recently, where I was asked at reception for my Direct Barring Services (DBS) certificate. This was not a problem as I always carry it with me if I'm visiting a school. However, I was also asked for photographic ID. Again, this was not a problem as I have my driving licence at all times (except bath time). The receptionist then went on to ask me if I had brought a utility bill that was less than three months old with me. I had never been asked for that and although my meeting had been arranged by email some weeks earlier, I had not been asked to bring such an item with me. Since I had failed to produce this document, the receptionist told me that I would have to surrender both my DBS certificate and my driving licence for the period of my visit. I was then informed that as I had not brought all the correct documents I would have to wait in the lobby until a member of staff with responsibility for safeguarding could speak to me and sanction my admittance. I wasn't offered a cup of coffee or even a glass of water. Finally, after half an hour of waiting, I was admitted, but it didn't end there. I was informed that without a full set of documents I would have to be accompanied by a member of staff at all times. I was even escorted to the staff toilet by a male member of staff! They did, I admit, stop short of coming into the toilet with me, so that was a relief. (No pun intended!) Now, I have worked in and around schools for 30 years and I was headteacher for 15 years, so I do really understand the importance of safeguarding, but this all seemed a little heavy-handed and certainly did not make me feel very welcome.

By contrast, I recently visited a Roman Catholic secondary school. I have visited a number of Catholic primary schools but never a secondary one and so I was particularly looking forward to this visit. My experience could not have been more different. I was greeted by the receptionist with a smile, and she made some quip about the parking (or lack thereof) around the school. This was actually quite disarming. Yes, of course, she verified my DBS number and my photo ID and rightly so. I was quite early for my appointment, but I was offered coffee, given a comfortable seat in a waiting area and was invited to join them for assembly. And no, before you ask, I was not accompanied to the toilet.

Two very different schools, which were trying to educate young people to become fully functioning members of society, but with a very different feel and different priorities.

Whilst the purpose of schools is broadly the same wherever you go, their 'sense of purpose' can be quite different.

Time to reflect

- If a visiting parent or an Ofsted inspector asked you to briefly summarise what your school's sense of purpose is, what would you say?

- What do you think one of your classroom teachers might say?

The school business manager?

The office receptionist?

A teaching assistant?

Chair of governors?

Site manager?

(Please note, this list is not in any kind of priority order!)

- If you had to score the alignment of the answers of the above people with your own on a scale of 1 to 10 (with 10 being high), what score would you give?
- What are the implications for your leadership team and particularly for you as a school leader?

Ten years ago, the phrase 'mission statement' was very much in vogue in schools. There was an expectation that Ofsted would expect to see such a statement in clear evidence around school. (I'm not sure, in all honesty, whether this was a requirement or an urban myth and as I can think of nothing more excruciating than reading old inspection frameworks and schedules to find out, I'm going to take a punt that it was a requirement at the time!)

I diligently produced something suitable and memorable. Please note the use of the word 'I' because although my then assistant head worked wonders with the graphics and Microsoft publisher (which is beyond my limited IT skills), I don't recall involving anybody else in its creation. If I am correct in this, then it was a huge mistake and an opportunity missed because how could I expect other people to buy into a statement about the school's sense of purpose when they had not had the opportunity to contribute? It certainly meant something to me, but however many copies we put up around school (in the classrooms, reception area, corridors, halls – it was a big school, so there must have been dozens of the things!), I am not sure it was very meaningful to the majority of staff or, indeed, the pupils.

To be honest I could only remember what one of the letters stood for as I was writing this. That was 'V' for valuing staff. I guess that I am kind of proud that this is the one that I can remember as treating staff well is so important in any organisation. Fortunately, my friend and former colleague, who is far more organised than I, retains a copy. This is how it read:

Positive self-esteem
Opportunities for all pupils to succeed
Standards of behaviour and attainment that are high
Involvement of parents and community
Teamwork
Innovative teaching
Valuing *all* staff
Enjoyment and a love of learning
Secure environment

Laudable, but over-long and contrived in places. Many schools now seem to take the initials of the school name to create something shorter and more memorable. For example, Helmworth Primary School may become **H**appy, **P**roud and **S**uccessful. There is certainly something to be said for 'the power of three' provided that it truly reflects the values of the school and not just three convenient words chosen to fit.

Above all, I believe that schools' distinct characters help drive that sense of purpose. As children and pupils ourselves in the past, would it not have been so boring if all teachers operated in the same way rather than displaying their distinct personalities? This is what schools do so well in general. They are distinct places shaped by the personalities of the people who lead them.

I was talking recently with Kim Johnson, the outgoing president of the National Association of Head Teachers (NAHT). He was once asked by a parent, 'How do I choose a school for my child?' He replied that you should trust your instincts about the personality of the headteacher. He and I both believed in showing round new parents wherever possible. Kim advised the parent to try to meet the headteacher and look for one who had spark and may even be a little cranky: a real character, with a passion for their school. In the same way that dogs become like their owners, schools become like their leaders over time! Kim's own children attended a very small primary school. It was clear to the teachers at secondary school which primary school these children had attended because they *all* knew a little Shakespeare and could *all* play a musical instrument. Schools are not sausage factories; they are unique and reflect the values and sense of purpose of all the staff that work there – a sense of purpose that everyone needs to buy into.

Vision in action

So what can a school leader do in order to build a vision for their school? Start by thinking about the following:

- **Capture** – A vision statement should capture the culture of your school, not define it.
- **Clarity** – Is there a real vision and clarity around what your school is trying to achieve?
- **Communication** – If you were to ask a teacher, teaching assistant, child and parent what the school stood for, would they broadly say the same thing (albeit in slightly different language)? Audit, and find out.
- **Coherence** – Schools tend to project outwards, often concentrating on the image they give out to parents and inspection teams, and of course to the children. Do we spend too much time selling the image to the outside?
- **Convince** – You have to make your teaching and non-teaching staff 'feel it' before you can convince anyone else, and this requires a significant investment of time and energy.
- **Leadership** – The challenge for school leaders is to create the conditions that create clarity and coherence.

In addition to defining the school's sense of purpose, you need to model the behaviours that will lead to the vision in action. For example, you can't expect staff to be creative and take risks if you don't take risks yourself. Also, you can't expect the children to be creative and take risks if they do not see the teachers doing that.

Vision in action requires a lot of time and energy. It cannot be a bolt-on, nor can it be something you create on your computer and then laminate. A vision is only successful if it becomes the culture of the school.

Authentic school cultures are hard to build but easy to destroy. A midday supervisor screaming at the kids on the playground can do untold damage to the vision. It is all about behaviours and ensuring all staff embody these behaviours at all times. The starting point is what do we want the children to look like as human beings when they leave us? Create a blueprint for this and you create a blueprint for staff (and parents!). Start from there and then work back.

Summary

- We all need a clear sense of purpose in order to function effectively and to thrive.
- A sense of purpose is closely linked to a sense of hope.
- Having a sense of purpose is also linked with longevity.
- Without values, individuals and schools have no moral compass on which to base their decision making.
- A school-based sense of purpose is something that all staff need to buy into. The best leaders listen as much as they speak.
- A vision is only successful if it becomes the culture of the school.
- Authentic school cultures are hard to build but easy to destroy.

2 Optimism

Optimism is the most important human trait because it allows us to evolve our ideas, to improve our situation, and to hope for a better tomorrow.

Seth Godin (2010)

In over 25 years of teaching, I was lucky enough to work for some truly inspirational school leaders and whilst they were all very different people who brought their own distinct personalities to the role, they shared a common trait: optimism. This is our second balloon that we sometimes need to work to keep inflated.

Let me begin by asking you this question: are you an optimist or a pessimist?

I guess in our heart of hearts, most of us would prefer to be considered an optimist. We tend to think of optimists as being popular, gregarious types – the kind of people you might want to include in any fantasy dinner party guest list (my guest list, by the way, would include the late Professor Stephen Hawking and Mel Giedroyc of *The Great British Bake Off* fame – you know, when it was on the BBC and really good!).

By contrast, we often think of pessimists as people who are the harbingers of doom. Let's face it, if you were allowed to select the members of your year group team, you would hardly be likely to shout out, 'Let's have Rebecca, she's really pessimistic!' I kind of imagine pessimists as the sort of people that you might well take a swift detour into a stockroom to avoid when you spy them coming down the corridor with the demeanour of Eeyore from *Winnie the Pooh*.

Time to reflect

Who have been the three most inspirational leaders you have met in your career so far?

1

2

3

Where would you place each individual on a scale of 1 to 10, where 1 is highly pessimistic most of the time and 10 is highly optimistic most of the time?

1

2

3

Now I am not really a betting man, but I would stick my neck out and say that the leaders who have inspired you are likely to score highly in terms of optimism.

Inspirational leaders, in my experience, are optimists and are infectiously positive and generally enjoy life, and, if we want to be resilient, optimism is most certainly a balloon we need to keep inflated.

So what is optimism?

Optimism can be defined as a tendency to look on the more favourable side of life's events. It is a disposition, if you like, in which the individual expects favourable outcomes.

Optimism is closely associated with words such as hopefulness, cheerfulness and confidence.

Optimistic school leaders will likely encounter as much adversity as anyone else, but will tend to see that adversity as a challenge to be overcome and may even derive satisfaction from attempting to conquer it. Of course not all challenges can be overcome, and setbacks and failure will punctuate every school leader's career. However, optimistic leaders tend to see failure as a temporary state.

> *If you believe it will work out, you'll see opportunities. If you believe it won't, you will see obstacles.*
>
> Dr Wayne Dyer (2010)

There is evidence that an optimistic approach can be good for you. One such benefit is that it can improve physical health (Mayo Clinic, 2017). It can:

- increase your life span
- improve your immune system
- reduce the risk of cardiovascular disease
- help build better coping skills during times of hardship or stress*
- improve your psychological and physical wellbeing.

*NB: There is no one definition of stress. Some psychologists argue that there is such a thing as good stress, whilst others make a distinction between pressure and stress. This is my view: we all need some pressure in our lives. Without it, we become bored and demotivated. However, too much pressure will cause a stress response, which can be damaging both physically and mentally. If we adopt that understanding of stress, then it is dangerous to our body as well as our mind. Increased levels of stress can be linked to high levels of inflammation, weaker immune systems, increase in headaches and other symptoms.

And pessimism?

Pessimistic people tend to see the meaning of life's events to be inherently negative and discouraging.

If this thinking becomes habit, it develops into what Dr Martin Seligman describes as 'learned helplessness'. Helpless people will see events as being out of their control and so whatever they do, it will have little or no

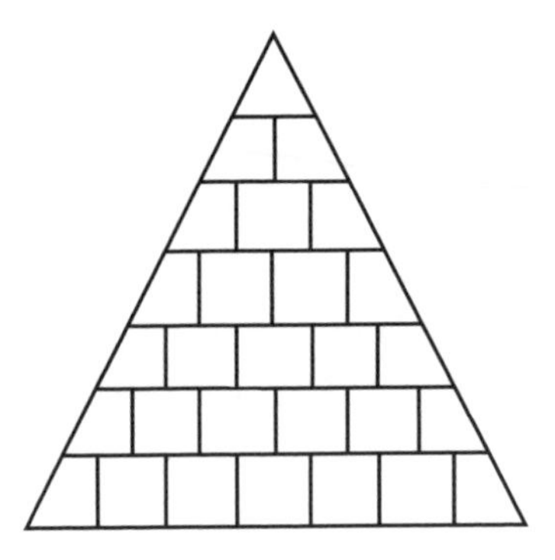

Figure 1.1 The structure of pyramid thinking

impact. Such thinking can lead to apathy and apathy can have no place in the modern school. Pessimism has also been linked with psychological conditions such as depression, damaging levels of stress, and anxiety (Kamen and Seligman, 1987).

Kim Johnson, formerly President of the National Association of Head Teachers, once said to me that pessimists in schools have a tendency to be 'pyramid thinkers' – they find obstacles to any new development or initiative and when these are removed, they always uncover a layer of larger obstacles hidden beneath.

> One pyramid thinker I used to work with was a teacher called Marion. Marion was lovely, but a bit of a pessimist. She had been teaching a long time and had seen it all! With any new development or initiative, Marion would always find an obstacle or problem. I always believed that as a school leader, it was my job, where possible, to remove obstacles to people teaching effectively. The difficulty with Marion, though, was that as you removed the top stone of the pyramid, she would then discover another layer of larger obstacles underneath. Remove those and there would be another layer beneath and so on. I eventually realised that I could not take ownership of all Marion's obstacles and objections and that she was uploading her difficulties on to me. I had to challenge her and say, 'I understand your problem, Marion. Now what can *we* do together to help overcome it?' She began to take some ownership eventually and became more solution-focused.

You will be familiar with the effect that pessimistic teachers can have on a school's creativity and innovation. To be an innovative teacher, you need to be wide open to ideas and see possibilities rather than barriers. You need to be willing to take risks in order to improve your teaching. You need to have a sense of adventure and an expectation of success. Those who have a pessimistic outlook typically approach changes to the status quo with the familiar, 'We tried this approach 15 years ago. It didn't work then and it won't work now.' These are the people that David Taylor, author of *The Naked Leader*, describes as 'negs' (Taylor, 2002). He calls them 'the disciples of doom'. They love to point out why things are doomed to failure. As individuals they hang around in the corner moaning, but when they come together they become a powerful force of negative energy. These people often label themselves in staff meetings as 'devil's advocate'.

I used to work with a teacher called Tom. Tom was not a glass-half-empty kind of a person. As far as Tom was concerned, he hadn't even been given a glass! He would find the flaw in every good idea and had also been around long enough to have seen everything before. 'It didn't work then and it won't work now!' He always believed he was given the worst class in school and the least amount of resources. You know the type of person I am talking about. We have all encountered them. Andy Cope and Andy Whittaker in their book *The Art of Being Brilliant* (2012) refer to such people as 'mood-hoovers' on account of their ability to suck the energy out of the room. Most 'negs' are glass-half-empty people. You will never completely change them but as a leader you can try to work out how to make their glass a little fuller, one drop at a time.

> *If you think that you can do something or think that you can't you're probably right.*
>
> Henry Ford

Most teachers understand that having an optimistic attitude is an important element in teaching effectively. However, having a positive outlook is much easier when everything is going well. These are challenging times in education and unfortunately when we come across an obstacle, pessimism can become a more dominant voice inside us and can potentially short-circuit our chances of reaching our goals.

Martin Seligman identified three components of pessimism that hold us back when things don't go right (Seligman, 2018). So, what are the three Ps of pessimism?

1. Personalisation

The first component of pessimism is personalisation. There are two aspects to this.

The first is when our inner voice tells us that we are not good enough and that we will never amount to anything. Many teachers feel like that at some point in their career. Even when I was head of a very large and successful primary school, I would sometimes come away from cluster heads' meetings feeling inadequate because other people seemed so much more knowledgeable than me. When we get into this way of thinking, we often believe obstacles are there because of us. 'Everything is my fault' is a common belief. In fact, when something goes right, pessimists will often refuse to take credit for it and will just put it down to being lucky on that occasion.

The second aspect is when, as a leader, you take negative interactions personally. A random call or visit from an angry parent can impact on our view of ourselves and our self-worth. In a career spanning nearly a quarter of a century in senior leadership roles in schools, I had many such visits and yet, looking back, I can only recall two or three sets of parents that had a problem with me personally. The rest of the time, it was because of the seat that I sat in and had someone else been sat there, they would probably have had the exact same encounter. As a leader, it's not always about you. This doesn't give you an excuse to be overly harsh or insensitive to the needs of others, but sometimes the reactions of other people have more to do with *their* circumstances than what *you* have contributed to the situation.

Time to reflect

Think of an occasion recently when something did not go right for you either at work or at home.

- What happened?
- How did you feel?
- How did you react?

- What was the outcome?

- How might someone who was not emotionally attached to the circumstances have reacted differently?

Sometimes, things just don't go right in school. It's not a grand conspiracy theory against you as a leader, it's just the way life works. It is, of course, easy to say but try to avoid taking setbacks personally, but rather, channel your energy and time on finding ways to overcome them.

2. Permanence

Optimistic people generally believe bad events and setbacks to be more temporary in nature than permanent. They tend to bounce back quickly from failure, whereas pessimistic people take longer periods to recover or may never recover at all. Optimists point to specific temporary causes for negative events; pessimists tend to see failure as permanent.

Dev was a good teacher, in my view. He had joined the school where I was then deputy head, as a newly qualified teacher. He had interviewed well and had come with excellent references from the university where he had completed his PGCE. He was motivated and popular amongst staff and pupils. We taught together in an area of a building constructed in the 1970s, where there were three Key Stage 2 classes located in an open-plan area. It was far from ideal, not least because the children on the periphery of each class had no dividing walls to block the sights and sounds of the other classes and, as such, would find themselves tuning into whichever was the most interesting lesson at the time!

Dev had been saddled with a weight of expectation from his university. He was labelled as an outstanding student. The reality is that there is a difference between being an outstanding *student* and an outstanding *teacher*.

We are all learning throughout our teaching career and although he had huge potential, he inevitably had a great deal to learn. He did well enough in his first lesson observation by his mentor, but it was not an outstanding lesson. Nor was the lesson observed by our headteacher at the time. There were plenty of positives as well as some areas for development. As the year wore on, Dev became more and more focused on the areas of development (or the negatives, as he saw them). He became more anxious about observations. He took feedback and setbacks and started making them permanent rather than something he could learn from. 'I'm never going to teach an outstanding lesson,' he used to say, and his confidence began to plummet.

We all engage in faulty thinking and need someone who is more objective and less emotionally involved to challenge our perceptions of ourselves. One day after school, Katie (the other teacher who taught alongside Dev and myself) and I sat down with him and talked through the many great things we saw in his teaching and contribution to school life each and every day, and gradually he began to get his mojo back. I don't know where Dev works now, but I imagine that with experience he went on to become that outstanding teacher that he always set out to be.

'I will never be able to do this' or 'I always get it wrong' are phrases used by the pessimist in us.

I used to work with a teacher called Joanne, who I found very difficult to manage. 'She is always so negative,' I would grumble. Truthfully, looking back, it wasn't always, only sometimes. The fact is, the words *never* and *always* are unhelpful when it comes to maintaining a resourceful attitude during challenging times. If you catch yourself saying, 'I'll never be able to achieve that', make sure that you try to challenge yourself on this false assumption. If you are struggling to challenge yourself, then find someone who can.

Time to reflect

Who do *you* turn to in order to challenge your inner voice when you are doubting yourself?

1 At school?

2 At home?

3. Pervasiveness

It sometimes feels as though if one thing goes wrong, then it impacts on every other aspect of our lives. This is known as pervasiveness. We all think that way from time to time, but for pessimists it is a prevalent way of thinking.

For example, you spill coffee over yourself at breakfast in the morning, so you have to get changed. You are late leaving for work and get snarled up in traffic where every traffic light decides to turn red on you. You arrive at school flustered and not in the best of moods. To cap it all, the photocopier is not working! Your mood is likely to last for the rest of the day. It impacts on your work, your relationships with pupils, other staff and your family at the end of the day. One event affects your overall happiness that day.

The importance of optimism in school leadership

Optimism is an essential trait for anyone working in a school, but particularly in school leaders. A word of warning about optimism though: people who are unfalteringly optimistic, whatever the situation, run the risk of appearing a little bit fake or plastic. It is also likely to p**s other people off and earn you a reputation as being deranged and living in 'la-la land' (by the way, am I the only person who did not get that film?).

The case for optimism as an essential trait in school leaders is clear.

- Optimistic leaders bring an energy and passion that helps to attract the best talent to their schools.
- Optimistic leaders are more resilient and bounce back quicker when faced with setbacks and failure.
- Over time staff become more like their leaders. (In other words, grounded optimism spreads in varied measures to both staff and pupils.)

Whilst I do strongly believe that the best school leaders are optimists, optimism does come with a health warning. Optimism needs to be tempered with realism, otherwise we can become blinded to the dangers or risks of our chosen course of action. I think optimism and kindness pretty much go hand in hand. Sometimes school leaders will struggle with balancing kindness and empathy with holding people to account. I know it was a weakness of mine at times. As such, we sometimes experience an inner struggle between knowing a difficult conversation needs to be had and knowing it may upset the positive vibe around school, as inevitably people talk. We can drift into blind optimism; hoping that the situation will improve. Clarity of expectation flies out of the window and people become unclear about what is needed from them. As a result, performance goes down, the children suffer and results will most likely take a dive.

Remember that true optimism is different from blind optimism. Optimism is about being positive about achieving a desired result when there are obvious gaps in structure, plans, infrastructure, etc. that are needed to achieve it. Blind optimism is when you believe that nothing bad can happen. This can lead to overconfidence and naivety, disappointment or even danger. For example, I was driving over to see my mother in Leicester recently, which is a 70-mile round trip from Derby where I live. I forgot to check the petrol gauge and around five miles into my journey the petrol warning light came on. The in-car computer told me I had 20 miles of travel left. I had to come off the M1 to fill up. To have carried on in the hope of arriving would be blind optimism in action. Similarly, receiving an unsatisfactory inspection report and hoping, as a senior leadership team, that 'things will just work themselves out', would be blind optimism indeed! True optimism doesn't just ignore challenges or pretend that negative feelings and experiences don't exist.

I recently met up with Kim Johnson. Kim introduced me at the NAHT Education Conference in London in 2014 and it was clear to both of us that we shared the common belief that you cannot build and sustain a school without putting staff wellbeing, as well as that of the pupils, at the centre of it. Over a cup of coffee at St Pancras station in London, we got to talking about optimism.

'Optimism is fundamental for school leaders,' he said and I agreed. If we cannot bring ourselves to believe in the potential of children to achieve, then what chance do they have? Many do not have that belief in themselves and do not always get the support and encouragement to aspire within their home environment. However, Kim went on to point out that it is not the duty of senior leaders to be optimistic on behalf of others. It is the duty of all teachers to be optimistic. Most enter the profession full of hope and belief that they can make a difference. Sadly some, over time, lose that spark and vitality and pessimism takes a hold. It is not the profession for everyone and for some the decision to leave is the right one.

A headteacher friend of mine, Peter, had a brilliant deputy for many years, Amanda. They made an excellent team with a shared vision and the seeming ability to finish one another's sentences, but eventually Peter started to notice a gradual change in Amanda. She started to arrive a little later in the morning and seemed to have lost some of the bounding energy and enthusiasm for which she was known. Then, one morning she called in sick with nausea and headaches. After a couple of days of feeling this way, Amanda went to see her GP. Her husband, Mark, went with her. She was signed off for a month. During this time Peter sent flowers and a card. He tried emailing her to ask if there was anything he could do to help and support. Perhaps he might come and visit her? He received no reply. Peter tried texting and calling her mobile but it remained switched off.

Eventually he tried ringing Amanda's landline number. There was no reply in the daytime, so Peter tried again that evening. Mark answered. Peter had known him for years, but this conversation was different, awkward and stilted. Her husband said she was a little better but was still having some bad days and some sleepless nights. He asked Peter not to try to contact her directly but to come through him. Peter was, needless to say, devastated by this request. He felt hurt as though someone had chopped off his right arm.

The following week, Mark rang Peter to ask if he and Amanda could make an appointment to come and see him the following week at the end of the school day when staff would have gone home. It all seemed very formal but a meeting was set up for 6.45 the following Wednesday. Peter struggled to concentrate that day and largely got through on autopilot.

They arrived and Peter ushered them in, kissing Amanda on the cheek and shaking Mark by the hand. It all felt a little awkward.

Peter asked her how she was. 'Peter, I have decided to leave,' she said. 'I have loved working with you at this school over these last years, but I feel that the time has come to move on.' Mark explained that Peter was not the only one who had noticed a change in Amanda's behaviour over the last few months. 'I feel like I am losing my Amanda,' he said, 'and I want her back.' Peter recognised that nothing he could say was likely to change her mind. Amanda said that she felt ready to come back to work. She would not leave him, or the school, in the lurch and she would see out the two terms to the end of the academic year in order to give them time to find a suitable replacement. A measure of the person she was.

Amanda returned to work for those two terms as though a weight had been lifted. Her smile and enthusiasm had returned. The decision was made. For her, and actually for the school, the time was right.

For those two terms, Peter got his Amanda back and Mark got his Amanda back too.

Everything has its time.

Portuguese proverb

Optimism is a powerful tool that can have huge benefits in your personal life, but it is also a trait that can get you ahead in your career and help you be a really effective school leader. You would not be where you are in your teaching career if you did not have at least optimistic tendencies, but there is much to be gained in cultivating your optimistic outlook.

I can think of few places where optimism is more important than in leading a school; after all we are shaping the lives of the next generation. Really effective school leaders have a transforming effect on their staff and pupils. This is born out of the ability to convince others that they have the ability to achieve levels of performance beyond those they had previously thought possible. Such leaders are able to paint a picture of the future of the school that is optimistic. This, in itself, is not the difficult part. Most school leaders can engage in 'blue sky thinking'. The real skill is making that picture seem attainable in the eyes of staff and pupils. It is the ability to move other people from being stuck in the 'this is how things have always been done around here' and enable them to see 'how things could be done better'.

Warren Bennis, author of *The Leadership Advantage*, said that optimism is one of the key things people need from their leaders in order to achieve good results (Bennis, 1999). Whilst not writing specifically about education, I believe that it really does apply to the success of schools.

[Every] exemplary leader that I have met has what seems to be an unwarranted degree of optimism – and that helps generate the energy and commitment necessary to achieve results.

Warren Bennis (1999)

In times of difficulty or crisis in school, staff will usually turn to their leaders. They are not necessarily expecting them to have all the answers (at least not in the short term); sometimes all they want is a dose of hope. Hope is an emotion that can ebb and flow. It requires both leaders and others to make good choices in order to sustain its positive impact. As such, the school culture and relationships are vital of course, but many just want to hear a leader tell them that everything is going to be fine. They want a sense of security, a feeling that their worries will soon be over. They will look for hope to recapture that moment in time when they felt their best at work. The development state of schools is such that you are either solving a problem, coming out of a problem or heading into a new problem. Give them hope, by all means, but without action that hope will be transitory and soon dissipate.

Truly optimistic leaders and their schools combine hope, vision, values and actions.

How to maintain optimism as a school leader

The good news is that the three components of pessimism identified by Martin Seligman and noted above (personalisation, permanence and pervasiveness) are all learned behaviours that can be unlearned! So any teacher can replace them with more optimistic habits.

Martin Seligman argues that anyone can make use of learned optimism, regardless of how pessimistic their general outlook on life might be (Seligman, 2018). When we meet adversity, we react by thinking about it, often ruminating on the issue. It isn't long before our thoughts turn into beliefs and often become so habitual that we don't even know we have them. They can make the difference between dejection and giving up, and constructive action that contributes to our wellbeing.

Pioneering psychologist Albert Ellis said that it is a matter of ABC: Adversity, Belief, Consequence (Ellis, 1994):

- **Adversity** – Your best friend is not returning your calls.
- **Belief** – They don't value your friendship.
- **Consequence** – You feel rejected and depressed.

Seligman created a system based on Albert Ellis's ABCs in order to treat pessimism (Seligman, 2018). His revised system, ABCDE, is this:

- **Adversity** – The event that causes us a stress response, e.g. unfavourable feedback from a lesson observation.
- **Belief** – This is how we interpret the event, e.g. I am not good at my job.
- **Consequence** – The resulting action from the belief caused by the adversity, e.g. low mood and confidence.
- **Disputation** – Using evidence to challenge negative thoughts from A–C, e.g. an outside perspective from another colleague, revisiting more positive performance management reviews or thank you cards from parents.*
- **Energising** – Once you are able to shift yourself into more positive thoughts in response to A–D you end up feeling more energised and confident.

*When I find myself facing adversity, I try to use disputation and find another way of looking at the situation, e.g. I lost a booking to speak at a conference recently.

I felt a sense of rejection, but when I read the email through, it wasn't anything to do with me. The conference was cancelled due to unforeseen circumstances. Conference speaking is my bread and butter, so my initial reaction had been 'Oh ****!' But I asked myself if there was another way of looking at the situation and came to the conclusion that with travel times and an overnight stay, I had got two more free days in my diary. Two more days to work on this book before my deadline! Of course, I would take a financial hit but I instantly felt better and more energised and focused. Now I admit that sometimes I am better at disputation than others. Sometimes, I need outside help to do this.

As a speaker and author, Paul McGee (2012) would put it this way: we all need 'cheerleaders' and 'challengers'. Cheerleaders are people who will boost our egos. If I want my ego massaging (and we all do need that sometimes!), I will ring my mum. She thinks I am the best thing since sliced bread. However, she's my mum and not particularly objective. I'm half a loaf at best! So, if I want an objective opinion, I will ring my former co-head. She will not always tell me what I want to hear, but she will always give me an objective view and encourage me to look at a problem from a different angle.

Seligman's ABCDE technique has been widely used to treat pessimism in children, but it works well for adults too and has certainly helped me in challenging circumstances. Try putting it into practice yourself with the following exercise.

Time to reflect

Think of a challenging issue you are dealing with currently in school.

- Adversity
- Belief
- Consequence

- Disputation

- Energising

It would be glib to suggest that this technique will solve all your leadership challenges, but repeated use of it can help to raise your confidence levels and your mood.

Optimists don't have a special 'get out of jail free card' that magically exempts them from stress, but they do seem to manage stress more efficiently than others. Rather, they have a way of dealing with stress so that the stress disappears at a faster rate than pessimists.

Of course, there is a danger that we tend to categorise people as being either one thing or another: an optimist or a pessimist. Truthfully though, it is not a matter of polar opposites; we all exist somewhere on a spectrum between the two. There will be times as a school leader when you will feel more optimistic than others. These are, after all, very challenging times in education, with deep-biting cuts and another government initiative coming along at what seems like every month.

My message is this: it is okay not to feel optimistic 100 per cent of the time. You cannot keep that balloon fully inflated permanently. Don't beat yourself up about it. However, be aware that your mood does and will permeate out to other staff, so if pessimistic thinking becomes your norm, it will have a serious impact on your school. Try not to be harsh on yourself. Isolate the inevitable mistakes that we all make from time to time. Take what lessons you can from them and ensure that you're not falling into the trap of giving up on your goals.

What we see depends mainly on what we look for.

Sir John Lubbock

There is much truth in this quote. If we are looking for the negatives in school leadership, they are there in abundance. If we are looking for the positives, they are there too, but we sometimes have to dig a little deeper to find them.

Whilst staff need optimistic leadership, it is inevitable that your reserves of optimism are going to feel somewhat depleted at times. 'Stuff happens' and leadership roles can be rather lonely, to say the least. So let's look at five simple steps to help you boost your levels of optimism.

Five tips for maintaining personal optimism

1. **Avoid negative people** – No, don't laugh! If you have 'negs' on your staff, clearly you can't avoid them! However, I would always pick who I sat with at headteachers' meetings and on courses very carefully. Some people were serial moaners and complainers and had the ability to suck the energy right out of you. Whilst avoiding cries of favouritism, do try to seek the company of positive individuals in your school.
2. **Remind yourself of your strengths** – Boasting has negative connotations socially, but when we do it internally it can help to silence our negative inner voice. Most of us find it difficult to do this, so try writing a list of your triumphs and achievements. Keep it stuck inside your diary or planner, where no one else can see it, but look at it regularly if your optimism levels dip.
3. **Accept that you have limitations and there are some things you cannot change** – The following quote is often quoted, but whatever your religious beliefs or convictions, they are some of the wisest words I have ever read:

   God grant me the serenity to accept the things I cannot change, the courage to change the things I can, and the wisdom to know the difference.

   Reinhold Niebuhr

   When faced with a difficulty or setback, unpick it, identify the aspects that you *can* influence and then draw up a plan and get stuck in, so that you feel more in control of the situation.
4. **Find an alternative way of looking at setbacks** – With a trusted colleague or friend, try to alter your perspective. However challenging this may be, look for hidden positives in a negative situation; in other words try to find the proverbial silver lining.
5. **Focus on others** – Think about friends and family. Pursue projects and interests outside of school that you enjoy. The easiest way to make ourselves miserable (and believe me I have been there!) is to become isolated and inward-looking.

Creating a culture of optimism

School leaders have a moral duty, however challenging the circumstances, to be optimistic for the sake of their staff and pupils. If a school leader is optimistic, this will naturally bring an energy and passion to the culture of the entire school.

To maintain this throughout the school, however, it is important to encourage all members of staff to maintain their own personal levels of optimism too. As we've seen earlier in the chapter, this can be challenging, as any staff team will have its fair share of 'pyramid thinkers' (see p. 30), particularly when they, or the school as a whole, are facing difficulties or obstacles. Share the above advice with your team to help them to maintain their own personal optimism and also try the following additional tips to help all teachers in your school retain a more positive approach to teaching.

Five tips for maintaining an optimistic staffroom

- **Celebrate your successes** – Lots of schools have celebration assemblies for the children. Try making a staff morning briefing on Fridays a celebration of what has gone well that week.
- **Know your staff's strengths** – The more you can align work to a staff member's strengths, the more energised and optimistic they will feel.
- **Let people 'in on things'** – Where you can and particularly on topics that are important to them, be open with your staff. Nobody likes to feel an outsider. Good-quality and regular communication is of paramount importance.
- **Show flexibilty** – Many members of staff are parents themselves and being able to attend their own children's class assemblies, sports days or nativities is worth its weight in gold.
- **Model a work–life balance** – You are human. Let them know you go home early one night a week. Use internal emails sparingly. Human contact is always better.

A pessimist sees the difficulty in every opportunity; an optimist sees the opportunity in every difficulty.

Winston Churchill

Summary

- Optimism is a tendency to look on the more favourable side of life's events.
- Optimism is closely associated with words such as 'hopefulness', 'cheerfulness' and 'confidence'.
- Optimistic school leaders tend to see adversity as a challenge to be overcome and failure as a temporary state.
- Blind optimism occurs when an individual believes that nothing bad can happen. This can lead to overconfidence and naivety, and it can lead to disappointment or even danger.
- Martin Seligman identified three components of pessimism that hold us back: personalisation, permanence and pervasiveness.
- Whatever our natural disposition, optimism can be learned.
- Optimism is one of the key things people need from their leaders in order to achieve good results.
- Optimistic leaders combine hope, vision, values and actions.
- Optimistic leaders bring an energy and passion that is infectious.
- We have a moral duty to be optimistic for the sake of the children and young people in our care.

3 Trust

He who does not trust enough, will not be trusted.

Lao Tzu

Our third balloon on our journey to resilience is trust. Trust can be defined as an expectation or belief that you can rely on somebody else's actions and not just their words. You believe that person has the good intentions to carry out any undertakings or promises.

When you look at it like that, it is difficult to imagine how schools can grow and move forward if trust is missing. How can you build a successful school if you believe that parties within it are prone to spreading rumours, subterfuge or even outright lying, are nodding in meetings and paying lip service to new ideas and initiatives with no intention of carrying them out?

One of the traits of successful school leaders, therefore, is the ability to inspire trust. More than this though, it is the ability to *give* trust in return.

Time to reflect

- Have you ever worked for someone who made a promise to you and then broke that promise?
- How did you feel?
- Were there any mitigating circumstances?
- What were the long-term implications for your professional relationship?
- What would you do if somebody in a position of power over you asked you to do something that you think is ethically dubious, but asked you to trust them?
- How would you feel?

The answers to these questions have a profound impact on the relationships that we, as school leaders, have with other staff.

I was talking to a young teacher after delivering a workshop on resilience at a TeachMeet a few months ago. She was clearly under pressure and very agitated. Her school had dropped from 'Good' to 'Requires Improvement' in a recent inspection but that was not so much the part of the conversation that struck me. She talked of low morale and increased workload, but she repeatedly used the term 'Management'. 'Management said they would do this but they haven't.' 'Management are making us do this…' It was as if 'Management' were a completely alien species in her eyes. It saddened me. Rather than galvanising the staff, the inspection judgement had split them into an 'us and them' mentality. Perhaps they were like that before; I don't know. Nor do I know what the other side of the story might be. What struck me though was that, at least from this teacher's perspective, there seemed to be a breakdown of trust between school leaders and their 'followers'. It was difficult for me to see how this school was going to be able to move on without *trust*.

Let's be honest, the teaching profession has taken a bit of a battering in recent years. Accountability has never been greater and I don't think that the vast majority of school leaders have a problem with that; children only get one chance at an education after all. What is regrettable is that the high levels of accountability are not matched with high levels of trust in the profession from politicians.

It is ironic that in a 2016 Ipsos MORI survey, which ranked the trustworthiness of 24 professions as viewed by the general public, teachers came out third highest after nurses and doctors. Politicians, to whom the profession is answerable, came out last, with only 19 per cent of people believing that they largely tell the truth (Ipsos MORI, 2016).

Even against this background, and perhaps even more because of it, the ability to establish and (where needed) restore trust is one of the most critical traits required of school leaders if their schools are to survive and thrive in the current political landscape.

It is not always easy though.

I can remember in my first year as a headteacher, some 20 years ago (blimey – that makes me feel old!), attending headteacher induction training. It was called 'HEADLAMP' back then, but I have absolutely no idea what, if anything, the letters stood for. As part of this, we went on a two-day residential course in a hotel in Buxton. It was sufficiently close to my school to get back if there was a major crisis but sufficiently far away to make it difficult to 'pop' back.

I had left the school in the hands of my new and relatively inexperienced deputy, Richard. I had invested in a mobile phone – my first. Not quite the size of a brick but not far off. I'm not even sure it had a texting facility (now I really do feel old!).

On one level, I really enjoyed getting to know other new heads and realising that they were facing many of the same challenges that I was. It was also a great opportunity to share ideas and let our hair down in the bar in the evening. However, I didn't really relax. I think I rang school four times over the two days and would check my phone every break to see if I had any missed calls to say that something had kicked off that needed my input. It was not that I actively distrusted Richard's capabilities; I just hadn't learned to trust them yet and that made my job more difficult and lonely.

Over the coming weeks and months, and as I got to know him better, Richard dealt with numerous dramas whilst I was out of school and did so calmly, firmly and with diplomacy. I often felt that he had dealt with situations as well (and perhaps sometimes better!) than I. It just took time.

I learned over 15 years to trust in the skills of some great senior leaders. After I returned from my breakdown in 2007, the local authority injected extra funding so that I could co-head the school (which had around 600 pupils by this stage) for a year with Wendy, my assistant head. Whatever happened when I was away from school, I knew that the situation would be dealt with in the best possible manner because over time I had learned to trust her judgement completely.

When I was applying for my first headship, the system of inspection in English schools was very different from today. Schools were inspected for a week, every six years, with two months' notice to prepare for the inspection! The system was heavily criticised as with that much preparation time some schools could paint a picture of themselves that did not truly reflect the quality of teaching and learning and the day-to-day running of the school. (Several deciduous forests were sacrificed to make sure that my classroom display boards looked at their very best!) Against this background, the general advice to new headteachers was to change nothing in your first year.

The argument went something like this:

'Until you have lived through a full calendar year of Christmas concerts, parents' evenings, sports days and summer fairs, you cannot fully understand the school. Use the first year to gather information, build relationships and trust. Then you can make informed decisions and avoid "throwing the baby out with the bath water"'.

Sounds a really tranquil process doesn't it? Like easing yourself into a warm bath!

Of course, the reality in the modern age is that we rarely have the luxury of time. I was once 'parachuted in' as acting head of a school that had gone into special measures and whose head had decided to retire at that point. The local authority and Ofsted were looking for rapid improvements. Time was not our friend!

New heads these days rarely have the luxury of time to draw up their plans. Expectations from parents and governors (and often Ofsted or Estyn) are high!

So how, as a leader, do you build trust quickly?

School leaders are often in a position of having to make rapid progress towards new goals at a time when there may be an atmosphere of fear and suspicion. You are not going to make that accelerated progress without securing the trust of your staff, so how do you build it quickly? Patrick Ottley-O'Connor is an expert at doing this and has plenty of good advice.

I first met Patrick at a Pedagoo Hampshire event organised by Martyn Reah, founder of #teacher5aday.

The event was similar to a very large TeachMeet but with keynotes and lots of smaller sessions running at the same time, giving delegates a wide range of choice. It was a great event that was packed out and I would thoroughly recommend it. I was there talking about my first book and had the privilege of hearing Patrick speak and got chatting to him afterwards. He has a really fascinating job.

To give Patrick his official title, according to LinkedIn, he is Executive Principal: EFAT and Director of Collaborative Leadership Ltd (EFAT is a family of schools in Bolton, Lancashire). By the time this book is published, I would not be at all surprised if that title has changed somewhat, as Patrick is an interim headteacher. He is often invited in to help schools who have found themselves in difficult situations turn things around. It may be a set of poor exam results or an unfavourable Ofsted report, but the situation has generally led to the departure of the headteacher, sometimes at very short notice. Consequently, Patrick often does not know where in the country he is going to be working until a few weeks before the start of an academic year. He rarely stays in a school for more than a year and tells his senior leadership teams on day one that this is the first day of his exit strategy. Time is not a luxury that Patrick has. Rapid improvements need to be made but that is not going to happen effectively unless he can establish trust. I went up to visit Patrick a few months ago to find out more.

Inevitably, morale is not always good in schools that find themselves in such situations. Staff members are often feeling a little bruised or downtrodden and some may well approach any change in leadership with a degree of scepticism.

'Building trust needs to start on day one,' Patrick said.

On the first day, he gathers the staff and asks them to spot the lie in what he is going to tell them about himself. He spends a minute reeling off various facts about his background, claims to fame, etc., and then asks them to guess.

'The correct answer? There is no lie. Everything I told you is true.'

Patrick has two big messages, which he shares with staff in a new school at the start of the year:

Big message 1

'I will be honest with you and tell you no lies, but I will not always tell you what you want to hear.'

He emphasised to me that in order to establish trust you need to show authenticity.

'Bad news is not like wine. It does not improve with age.'

He reminds staff of this:

Anyone who has never made a mistake has never tried anything new.

Albert Einstein

Big message 2

'There is an expectation of high standards – no excuses. We are going to be moving at pace.'

On the first day, Patrick also hands out a staff perception questionnaire asking three main questions:

1. What's the best thing about the school?
2. What's the worst thing about the school?
3. What piece of advice would you give me?

Staff feel listened to and that their contribution is valued.

As a new head 14 years ago, Patrick received a great piece of advice from his old primary school teacher, Dr Geoff Mawson MBE: 'A good leader is not a hero, s/he is a hero maker!'

For Patrick, being a school leader is about growing others and building the capacity for sustainable leadership. It's about helping staff to trust themselves again and get their mojo back! It is about them having faith in the senior leadership team and seeing their role as 'Barrier Removal Operatives'. School leaders should ask staff, 'What are the obstacles getting in your way that are stopping you from better teaching?' Patrick's current setting that I visited was a relatively new build, but it was built with many open plan spaces (which from my own experience are a real dread). Staff saw these as a barrier to learning. So, they built walls! In other settings, people simply need liberating from bureaucracy. Patrick would argue, 'Stop focusing on writing lesson plans and put the emphasis on teaching lessons.'

In our conversations, Patrick made it absolutely clear that the children come first. As Simon Sinek says, you always have to start with your **'Why?'** (Sinek, 2009). Students have only one chance at an education, but what was also crystal clear was Patrick's belief that you really *do* have to look after teachers if you want to improve outcomes for children.

'Look after yourself. Then look after one another and *then* you can make a real difference to the students.'

He is a big believer in work–life balance and how having realistic expectations helps to engender confidence, energy and trust. It is not about getting people to do more and more. It is about getting people to do less better. He emphasises that as leaders 'we have to be the change we want to see.' Patrick has only sent out 11 whole-school emails in the last 12 months and discourages staff from sending them too.

'Let them know you have booked a holiday at half-term because it then makes it clear that you are not expecting them to work all the way through their half-term either.'

Perhaps you could sum up Patrick's immediate approach to building trust as follows:

- **H**onesty
- **A**uthenticity
- **H**igh expectations
- **L**istening
- **E**mpowerment.

If I was clever, I would probably construct some mnemonic from these letters, but I am not, so feel free to make up your own!

I could add another element to Patrick's approach, and that is a sense of fun! More of this in Chapter 7 (p. 115).

Leadership without mutual trust is a contradiction in terms.

Warren Bennis (1999)

Inspiring trust in yourself as a leader

Stephen R. Covey was one of the world's foremost authorities on leadership. From the oval office, to the boardroom, to the school hall, Stephen taught the mindset, skillset and toolset found in *The 7 Habits of Highly Effective People*, his seminal work (2004a). A teacher at heart, he often taught: 'There are three constants in life: change, choice and principles.' He is admired around the world for his simple, yet powerful, universal teachings.

Trust is a trait of leadership that does not always come easily but the first job of a school leader is to inspire your staff to trust you as a leader. In order for staff to trust you, they need to have confidence in you. Stephen Covey argues that confidence is born out of the two 'Cs':

1. competence
2. character.

Both of the above are essential to successful school leadership.

Competence is about your capabilities, results and your track record. It involves other people's perceptions about whether you possess the knowledge and skills needed to do the job, along with the interpersonal skills and wisdom needed to succeed at it. No governing body is likely to appoint a senior leader without the evidence of good results and references. Similarly, members of staff tend to have more respect for a leader who 'knows their stuff' and can 'inhabit their world'. One regret that I have is that in my second headship, as the school grew and grew, I spent more and more time on admin and less and less time doing any actual teaching.

Character is about your motives, your intents with people, your perceived benevolence if you like – the extent to which you are believed to want to do good for staff and pupils. It is also about the perception of your integrity and the extent to which you follow ethical principles. Lose your integrity as a leader and it is pretty much game over!

I can distinctly remember the first INSET day in the September in my second headship. It was the largest group of staff I had ever seen. They were sat in a circle looking at me expectantly, trying to weigh me up. Nervously, I cleared my throat and offered them two pieces of advice:

1. I wear my heart on my sleeve. What you see is what you get.
2. Never give me the original document, always a photocopy, because I have a bad habit of losing things and it will end in tears.

People laughed and you could feel the tension dissipate, but as for trusting me? That was something that would need to be earned.

You simply cannot be an effective leader without trust.

Time to reflect

Think of a school leader you have worked for and admired. How did they engender trust in staff through:

- Competence?

- Character?

Engendering trust is, in fact, a competency that can be learned, applied, and understood. It is something that you can get good at, something you can measure and improve.

Stephen Covey (2009)

So how do the best school leaders build trust?

When I was a deputy head, my headteacher, Pam Underwood, whom I admired greatly and tried to model my leadership style on, bought me a book as the birth of my son Jonathan approached. It was called *The Sixty Minute Father* and written by Rob Parsons. It was full of advice for busy dads.

Three particular pieces of advice have stuck with me through the years.

1. No one has ever died wishing they had spent more time at work.
2. The relationship that you have with your children when they leave home at 18 is most likely the relationship that you will have with them for life.
3. Your relationship with your children is like a bank account. There will be deposits and withdrawals. Spending time with them and playing is a deposit. Criticising them would be a withdrawal.

Rob Parsons says that the key is to keep the relationship with your kids 'in the black' and not go overdrawn (Parsons, 2009).

I would not claim to have been the best father in the world by any means, and there were times when I was particularly stressed at work ten years ago when I certainly went into the red, but it is an analogy that has stuck with me and is also applicable to school leadership.

You are only human. You are going to make mistakes along the way. The key is to stay in credit with those that you lead. To be credible as a leader, you must make deposits and build credit with staff before they will 'buy in' to new initiatives and agree to being led in new directions.

Leaders who are more transparent and positive are more likely to have followers who trust them and rate them as effective leaders.

M. C. Bligh (2017)

Stephen Covey (2009) suggests that there are behaviours that will help leaders build and maintain levels of trust. I hope you are not superstitious because there are actually thirteen of them. (I, myself, am not superstitious. When you have lived in a house numbered 13 for 25 years, there is very little point in being superstitious!) Strap yourself in – here we go…

1. **Talk straight** – Don't hold your tongue. Make sure everyone in school knows what you stand for and what your expectations are. Be up front when things are not good. As interim head Patrick Ottley-O'Connor says, 'Bad news is not like a fine wine…'
2. **Demonstrate respect** – Be humble. I always knew that if I was off work for a week with flu – you know, proper man flu! – the school would carry on without me, but if my site manager or bursar was off then things would quickly grind to a halt. Power does not equate to importance. For every fault or criticism you find, offer two compliments. Keep your accounts in credit. People want to be in an optimistic environment where they feel valued. Also, people who feel respected and valued feel happy to do more than is generally expected. They are willing to go that extra mile, and that is a key component for success in any school.
3. **Create transparency** – I'm not suggesting that everyone should know your salary, your inside leg measurements or how you like your toast done, but no one likes to feel left out or that there are conversations going on behind their back that affect them. Members of staff who are kept informed and understand the part they need to play in delivering the best possible education for the children are, quite understandably, much more likely to trust their leadership team. When information is lacking, people will always fill the gaps with speculation, often of the wild and inaccurate variety! It's human nature. Speculation can quickly become 'fact' (fake news, ladies and gentlemen, fake news!). Be transparent in what you do where at all possible. Of course, you can't tell people everything; some things should and need to remain confidential but staff should never have to guess where you are coming from.
4. **Right wrongs** – As a leader there is little point in saying to staff, 'Trust me', if we continue to leave ever-growing trails of unadmitted mistakes, wrongs and disasters behind us. 'I'm sorry, I was wrong' actually does go a long way in terms of building and maintaining trust. However, actions will always speak louder than words. As a new leader, putting historical injustices right will also earn trust and credibility.
5. **Show loyalty** – Good school leaders will push staff to go beyond their comfort zones, but crucially, they are there to support them. If teachers are armed with your confidence in them, they are more apt to take on challenges and the risk of failure that go hand in hand with creativity and innovation. However, you can't spark real loyalty simply by telling your employees you trust them. Again,

it needs to be backed up by actions. Teachers who know their leaders 'have their backs' will not only take on bolder challenges, they'll also stay put when they stumble every now and then or when the going gets tough.

6 **Deliver results** – Results are very tangible – we either deliver, or we don't. Good results that are ethically achieved will often silence our critics. Poor results or results achieved by 'dubious methods' will have the opposite effect. Things will usually come back to bite you somewhere down the line. Unfortunately, it's the intangible things like personality issues that can often derail deadlines and have a negative impact on your results. As a leader, it's critical to be aware of any dysfunction in your team. One of the advantages of leading large primary schools was the ability to split up combinations of people that just did not work. If you do not have that luxury, consider what you can do to mitigate the situation.

7 **Get better** – Rest on your laurels and you will ultimately become irrelevant. These are two paths to avoid. Accept (and make sure that your staff know you accept!) that you are not the finished article as a leader. You, like them, will make mistakes along the way but you will also know that you will aim to learn from those mistakes and improve. If you are not growing, you are dying. As my first headteacher said to me, 'James, the day you stop learning about this job is the day you should quit!'

8 **Confront reality** – School leaders must walk a tightrope, balancing on the one hand being an optimist, a 'merchant of hope', and being sometimes the bearer of bad tidings.

Not everything that is faced can be changed, but nothing can be changed until it is faced.

James Baldwin

It often takes courage to speak up and rock the boat, shaking up a comfortable status quo in school.

9 **Clarify expectation** – The daughter of my friend Mark has recently started a new job. She is not very happy. Perhaps frustrated would be a better word to sum up how she is feeling. Laura is desperate to make a good impression in her new job, having relocated from the south of England. Her new job bears some resemblance to her old one (social housing), but is markedly different in some respects. The difficulty lies in the fact that it's a new role in the council so there is no peer support, and her line manager is also new in post and has a lot on his plate. Laura's frustration is born out of a lack of clarity of expectation.

Staff members need to know exactly what is expected of them. There is a job description, of course, which they would have received in their application pack. However, we all know that there are unsaid rules as to what is expected of staff in every school. What are the boundaries of your responsibilities? What falls within and outside the roles of the job? This goes beyond any job description. To get the best out of people and achieve strong working relationships, these must all be clearly understood and agreed to.

10 **Practise accountability** – Accountability is good in my book as long as it is accompanied with clear expectations and trust in the person you are holding to account. We owe our students the best education possible. They pass through our doors just once. Accountability, however, is more than just a test score; it is about monitoring and evaluating all the processes required for every student to achieve their best. These are pressured times, but it is very important to remind ourselves that as teachers, our ultimate goal is to raise aspirations and take all of our students to a place they did not think they could get to.

11 **Listen first** – I have a poor concentration span, I must admit. As a school leader there were many distractions – phone calls, emails, parents wanting to see me, and the inevitable knock on the door. I knew that blinking was supposed to be a sign of listening in conversations, so I blinked a lot! Often, though, I was waiting for a pause in order to get my point across! I suspect I was not alone in this.

Listening is a much-overlooked skill I suspect. There is sometimes a perception gap between what we think is going on in school and what actually is. Active listening (rather than just blinking) can help you steer clear of some perilous traps but (and this is a big but) it must be backed by the appropriate actions. Past NAHT National President, Kim Johnson, talking exclusively for this book, stated that we have one mouth and two ears for a reason:

As a leader you need to do twice as much listening as talking. Make it clear that you will listen to their ideas, reflect on them and that you may incorporate them but that when it comes to the crunch, you have to make the decisions and that they may not always like them.

12 **Keep commitments** – I have beaten myself up a little over the years as to how little teaching I did in my latter years of headship, when we had around 800 pupils in school. Though to be truthful, I had come to the conclusion, rightly or wrongly, that to make a commitment to cover someone's class

and then find that because of some crisis or other I wasn't able to do so, was actually worse. Not keeping commitments, no matter how justified the reason, ultimately damages credibility and trust. It was a real dilemma. Keeping our word can sometimes be very costly at times too. Of course, there's nothing wrong with asking to be released from a commitment for a good reason but if that is not possible, then we need to make good on the commitment.

13 **Extend trust** – Whatever you do, you will not build trust in yourself from your staff unless you show trust in them. Full stop.

Having said all this, school leaders need to achieve a balance. For example:

Behaviour 1: talking straight does not give us an excuse to be rude. It has to be kept in balance with **behaviour 2: showing respect**.

In fact, *any* one of these behaviours, pushed to the extreme, can become a weakness.

Of course, trust is a two-way street. Other people have to earn our trust, don't they? Some staff members will seem more trustworthy than others. Would that there was just a simple formula but there isn't. Trust is something we feel more than we think in other people.

Look, I know that you have all good intentions and high integrity as a leader, but does everybody know that? The idea that a member of staff may not trust these intentions would probably rankle you (at least a little bit).

Other staff are going to feel exactly the same way. If you withhold your trust and expect them to earn it by proving themselves over long periods of time, they are inevitably going to feel insulted, demeaned and disrespected. The response to not being given trust is to not give trust. That's how the law of reciprocity, otherwise known as 'what goes around comes around', works.

Viv Grant is a former primary headteacher and was one of the youngest heads in the country to turn around a failing primary school. Now as an executive coach and Director of Integrity Coaching, Viv works daily with others who have taken on school leadership roles. Consequently, Viv understands better than most what it takes for school leaders to overcome the often deep, hidden, inner struggles of school leadership.

Viv Grant, speaking to me for this book, talked about the importance of trusting yourself as a leader before you can inspire others to trust you.

Trust is everything. If we don't trust ourselves then leadership becomes a very insecure and lonely place. You need to trust yourself to make the right decision, but you also need to trust others. How can you have an honest conversation without trust?

Building trust: the golden rules

To build trust amongst your staff, remember these five golden rules:

1. **Always keep confidences where you can** – However, don't promise confidentiality if you are unsure whether you should keep the information from other people, e.g. performance or ethical issues.
2. **Give credit where credit is due** – Acknowledge the contributions of others. Be an advocate for other people.
3. **Never talk about other people behind their backs, unless you have something positive to say** – If you do, others will assume you're doing the same to them. Again 'what goes around…'
4. **Make sure your messages are consistent** – Don't say different things to different people in an effort to please.
5. **If you are asked a question, then give a complete and direct answer** – So, no smoke and mirrors. If you don't have the answer, don't try to bluff it.

> *Because trust is a relational concept that occurs between people, both leaders and followers play a critical role in creating, sustaining, destroying, and rebuilding trusting relationships.*
>
> M. C. Bligh (2017)

Trust is key, and the foundation of trust lies in credibility.

Summary

- Trust can be defined as an expectation or belief that you can rely on somebody else's actions and not just their words.
- Successful school leaders inspire trust. More than this though, they *give* trust in return.
- It is difficult to make rapid school improvement in the absence of trust.
- Encouraging and modelling a work–life balance helps to engender confidence, energy and trust.
- You need to trust yourself as a leader before you can inspire other people to trust you.

- As a leader, you must make deposits and build credit in 'your account' with staff members before they will 'buy in' to new initiatives.
- You can only build trust by demonstrating **competence** and **character.**
- Follow Stephen Covey's 14 steps for leaders to build and maintain trust, including talking straight and always being respectful.
- Be mindful of the law of reciprocity – what goes around comes around.
- Remember the five golden rules of building trust.

---

4 Courage

Physical bravery is an animal instinct; moral bravery is much higher and truer courage.

Wendell Phillips

And so to the fourth of our ten balloons of resilience: courage. I suspect that if you asked a group of people to summon up an image of someone who is courageous, you would get a wide variety of answers – great wartime leaders perhaps, or soldiers who risked all on the battlefield to save a wounded comrade. Some people may bring to mind a great athlete, who overcame the odds to become a gold medallist, or an innovative business leader such as Steve Jobs or Richard Branson, who dared to be different and broke the mould. Some people (though I suspect much fewer!) may even call to mind a famous politician. However, sadly, I strongly suspect that no one would be likely to call to mind an image of their friendly neighbourhood school leader. Perhaps it is that we associate courage with people being famous and operating on a national or international stage, whereas the vast majority of school leaders work at a local level with scant recognition for what they do.

If a school was appointing a new headteacher and asked parents, pupils and even governors what characteristics they were looking for in their new headteacher, I suspect that courageous would come a long way down the list after kind, firm, imaginative and aspirational. The fact of the matter is that courage is not a trait that is generally associated with school leaders. And yet we know different, don't we? With so many plates to keep spinning, I cannot imagine any school could get through an academic year, term, month or even a working week without courage.

So what is courage?

> *Courage is not the absence of fear, but rather the assessment that something else is more important than fear.*
>
> Franklin D. Roosevelt

Leadership can be scary at times. Fear of failure or humiliation goes hand in hand with the job. Courage is feeling fear but moving forward anyway. If you are waiting for fear to disappear before you take action or make a decision, you are going to be waiting a long time! You are allowing fear to paralyse you if you mentally visualise a perfect scenario in your head that feels 'safe', before you take action.

> *You can never cross the ocean unless you have the courage to lose the sight of the shore.*
>
> Christopher Columbus

Many of us are told throughout our lives to 'be courageous', but that isn't always easy. In fact, courage is often one of the most difficult traits to integrate into our leadership style. There are two main reasons for this. Firstly, being courageous means being willing to face fear and embrace uncertainty, and our self-preservation instinct does not approve of this one bit! Secondly, most of us will, at some time, defer something, hoping either that the situation will improve or that there may come more advantageous circumstances in which to address the situation. Perhaps it's the difficult conversation with a colleague that you are nervous to have, or a promotion that you are afraid to apply for. We sometimes feel fear and take no action, hoping that one day we will find the courage to finally do it.

As I've mentioned, I am writing this in a cottage in Aberporth in Wales overlooking the sea and we have endured crashing waves and

60-mile-an-hour winds, brought on by Storm Brian (honestly – Brian? Who thinks these names up?). Despite the storm force weather, or perhaps because of it, I find this the easiest place to write. I have space and can marshal my thoughts away from the many distractions at home. The beach is two minutes away and when I need a break from writing, I take Eddie, my loyal Golden Retriever, and watch the waves crashing onto the sand. Much of my first book was also written here, but I've actually been coming with family and friends for 20 years.

There is a stream that brings the rainwater down from the surrounding hills, through a ravine, to the side of the cottage and onto the beach, where it snakes its way across the fine sand and finally to the shore line, where the water is lost amongst the waves.

Over two decades, I have visited that beach in all four seasons and it has never looked the same twice. The rock formations, of course, are largely unchanged but the seasonal tides change the ridge, undulating sand markedly from visit to visit. The route of the stream alters too, to adjust to the altering sandscape. The stream will always take the line of least resistance to the sea.

Sometimes as a school leader, like the stream, it is easy to take the line of least resistance. It is tempting not to want to upset the status quo and to avoid the difficult decisions. You never know what is on the other side of a difficult decision and that can be scary. Staying in the known, even though you know that may not be the right thing to do, can feel more comfortable. However, that way will eventually lead to us being swallowed up in the waves.

Time to reflect

Can you think of a time when, professionally, you took the line of least resistance, rather than what you knew to be right?

- What were the circumstances?

- What did you do/not do?

- What was the outcome?

- How did you feel about yourself?

- Faced with the same circumstances, what would you do differently?

Effective school leadership requires courage

Over time, leaders create a culture within their schools both by the things that they say and do, but importantly also by things that are left unsaid and undone.

Courage needs to be demonstrated on two levels: day-to-day and on a strategic level.

Day-to-day courage

Firstly, courage needs to be demonstrated on a day-to-day basis, in your dealings with other people – parents, governors and staff in particular.

The decision around whether or not to exclude a pupil for their behaviour towards staff, for example, requires courage, whichever way you play it. An exclusion, be it temporary or permanent, usually results in some very unhappy or very angry parents. This must be handled. On the other hand, a decision not to exclude is likely to result in some very unhappy staff, who may feel unsupported. (It is easy to have an opinion on this, particularly if you are not the one who has to actually call the shots!)

Parents

The vast majority of parents I worked with in 12 years as a senior leader were kind and supportive, but it is a well-known adage that ten per cent of parents take up to 50 per cent of your time. I'm not sure about the percentages to be honest, but there were certainly weeks when that is what it felt like! Some parents think that they have a right to dictate and this has to be faced down.

I remember, a few years back, in the days before assessment without levels, when the father of Jessie, a girl in Year 6, was told by her class teacher at parents' evening that she really did not think it was in Jessie's best interests to sit the level 6 maths paper. Her father was strongly of the view that she should. The teacher's argument was that she was a solid level 4 and might with a fair wind tip over into level 5. Jessie lacked confidence, and her teacher felt that sitting the level 6 paper would be beyond her abilities and would damage her confidence further. Jessie's father argued that as all her immediate friends were sitting the level 6 paper, it would further damage her confidence if she did *not* sit it.

Both Mum and Dad made an appointment to come and see me. Mum did not say a lot to be fair, and Dad was polite but resolute. They knew their daughter better than we did and what we were planning on doing (or rather, not doing!) would damage her, was how his argument went. Having already spoken to the class teacher, I was of the view that she knew their daughter's educational ability best and I told them that I respected her professional judgement and backed her judgement.

I thought they had accepted my decision but the next day they asked for a copy of the school complaints procedure. They went through every stage of that complaints procedure over the coming weeks and I knew with each next step that they were not going to give up. Having been through a committee of governors and appeals to the whole governing body (who asked searching questions, as they should, but ultimately backed our decision), the time for the sitting of the level 6 paper came and went. We did not enter Jessie. But that was not the end of the matter. They wrote to their MP to complain about the school and she rang me to ask for the justification for my decision.

It was draining, to say the least, and although I never shifted in my opinion that supporting the class teacher's professionalism and judgement was the right thing to do, it took some courage to stick to my guns as the parents ramped up the pressure stage by stage. I was honestly expecting them to report me to Ofsted. If they eventually did then the complaint was not taken any further because I didn't hear from them.

I am far from being superhuman, and although I believed I was right, I confess that were times when I was close to buckling and letting them have their way. The temptation to go for the easy life was strong at times, but I'm glad that I didn't for three important reasons:

1. I believe, to this day, that it would not have been in Jessie's best interests.
2. The message that your leader will back you all the way unless s/he is in a corner severely damages relationships with staff. Once the genie is out of the bottle…
3. I could live with myself.

It was not the easiest thing to do but it was the *right* thing to do.

In common with many school leaders, I have over the years been verbally abused and threatened by parents, although I thankfully escaped any physical assault. Not everyone is so fortunate.

Around ten years ago, we were starting to see the negative impact of social media in schools. The start of the day was often being taken up with mopping tears and sorting out who said what about whom on Facebook or by text and then having to invite parents in to discuss the matter. They were often highly defensive, believing that their son or daughter could never have said such things… until confronted with the evidence!

These days, things have moved on a pace. The technology has of course become increasingly sophisticated and I am struggling to keep up with the wide variety of platforms available. My own kids laughed at me recently when I mentioned 'Facebook timing' someone! But it is not just the technology that has moved on in the last decade. School leaders are increasingly having to spend their time and energy sorting issues between parents that originate as comments on Facebook and the like, but which then spill over onto the playground. It is becoming far too common for parents to vociferously criticise a school through the perceived anonymity of Facebook or even to make vicious personal attacks on members of staff. Aside from the pain that this can cause, reputations can be damaged. These are the kinds of behaviours that the modern leader will inevitably need to confront day to day and that takes courage.

Governors

I have been lucky enough to have worked with some great and very supportive governors over the years, who have had my back in times of need. Nevertheless, however well meaning they may be, most do not come from an education background yet may have strong views based partly on perceptions and their experiences from their own time in school. I have also encountered a few (mercilessly few!) who were in it for self-interest rather than for the sake of the children, and a couple who were indiscreet and leaked confidential information to other parents, which led to rumours being spread. Sadly, I have also encountered one or two who were actually duplicitous. When your performance management and pay are determined by governors, it takes courage to stand up to them!

Staff

Many school leaders, I am sure, would say that it is better to maintain a professional distance between yourself and the staff members you lead, and as a rule of thumb I agree. However, as with most things, it's not always as easy as that.

> *Be warm in your engagement with staff but you do need to know when to pull up the drawbridge.*
>
> Kim Johnson

In my first headship, a large primary school, I was promoted to the position of headteacher upon the retirement of the previous incumbent who had mentored me, and whom I respected greatly. I had by this stage been deputy at the school for eight years and a classroom teacher for the whole of that time. It would have been difficult not to have forged friendships in that time.

Truth be known, it was both a blessing and a curse.

On the plus side, I had a substantial body of support from people willing me to do well and willing to go the extra mile in order to make sure that I did. Even the staff members I was less close to (not because I didn't like them but because the geography of the building meant that I had less to do with them on a day-to-day basis) seemed to take the view that it was 'better the devil you know'.

On the downside, if I distanced myself from my friends it might be interpreted as being 'stand-offish', as if power had gone to my head. On the other hand, I was very conscious that if I maintained those friendships I may be open to accusations of favouritism. It was a real dilemma.

Ultimately, I chose not to be distant from people, but I was always aware that it was harder to have 'difficult conversations' with friends and hold them to account. I always had to remind myself that the children come first.

I also knew that I had to strive to ensure that those I was close to had no more influence over my decision making than anyone else.

Not easy!

'There are all kinds of courage,' said Dumbledore, smiling. 'It takes a great deal of bravery to stand up to our enemies, but just as much to stand up to our friends.'

J. K. Rowling (1997)

Courage at a strategic level

As well as having the courage to face the day-to-day challenges of leading a department, subject or school, leaders need to demonstrate courage at a strategic level – for example, daring to be different to the other schools in your area.

When I first became a teacher in the late eighties, it seemed as though there were three or four initiatives a year being rolled out by the Department for Education and Science (DfES) as it was back then. At that time, this seemed a lot but now the pace of change is such that it probably seems more like three or four a month! Schools are like oil tankers; it takes them time to change course. Often it feels as though you set off in one direction only to find that, because of another new initiative, the destination has changed completely. My friend, Sam, worked as UK manager for a global technology company for many years. He got very frustrated at times because they would never complete one management restructuring before the next one came along. At times, school leadership can feel a little bit like that too.

Truth be known, you cannot slavishly follow every new initiative. What happened to 'Gifted and Talented'? When was the last time you heard anyone talk about the 'Every Child Matters' agenda? Sometimes a shortage of staff and resources or the physical layout of the building means that some initiatives are impractical to carry out. For example, the only external door to one of our Reception classrooms opened up on the school drive and was a fire door, which was kept locked for safety and security reasons. Free-flow indoor/outdoor play may have been desirable but it was completely impractical. It takes courage to stand up and say, 'Actually no, we are not going to do that.'

Ross Morrison McGill is a teacher and school leader with 23 years' experience. He has written three books on teaching and is passionate about teacher wellbeing and teaching and learning. In 2010, he founded @TeacherToolkit, one of the most popular websites for sharing resources and ideas around the world, and which has, at the time of writing, nearly 200,000 followers on Twitter. I recently asked him his thoughts on the importance of courageous leadership. This is what he said.

Courageousness has become an important trait of leadership in schools. We often assume that leaders are courageous – they make brave decisions and are always under pressure. This is often heightened when things go wrong or when safeguarding issues arise; or when a school is facing inspection. On my travels over the last four months, teachers cite marking as their greatest burden. School leaders, therefore, are obligated to remove things that are not necessarily required, simply because any teaching and learning policy is not a statutory requirement. For example, by removing a frequency from episodes of marking, e.g. three times a week, a school can free teachers up from monitoring by frequency, to evaluating by quality.

On the other hand, if you ask school leaders what their greatest workload issue is, they will tell you it is paperwork, and when you dig deeper, you'll find that what drives school leader workload is external accountability, or at least our perceptions of what is expected by our external partners.

However, for all the great, courageous decisions you might make to reduce workload, e.g. streamlining data systems or removing the burden of marking, if a group of inspectors decide to visit your school and make a very simplistic decision to measure the quality of what a school does based upon one fifth of its population, we have a problem. Decisions made in this way can influence the mood and perception of an entire community however courageous we might wish our school leaders to be. Thus, the way we are judged by external forces makes school leaders and therefore teachers jump through hoops. We all have to pay the bills at the end of the day, so we often default to do what is required rather than what we know is best for our colleagues and for our students.

The downside of all this external accountability is teacher wellbeing and mental health. There is often one person around that table who has lost their mojo; lost their way and often in need of reshaping – opting instead to be comfortable in where they work, their role, perhaps counting down the days to retirement. Some leaders can end up getting sloppy and a bit stuck in their ways. Others, you get the sense that they are there with a view to a quick win promotion and will do whatever is needed, including cutting other people down in order to achieve their goal. You find these aspects of leadership personalities in any business, but on the whole, the majority of school leaders I've worked with are there for the right reasons – the students.

The key is everything in moderation, including moderation. As a leader you need to achieve a fine balance. You cannot say you are really brave or really scared. We are all a bit of both, depending on what is going on around us at any one particular time. Ask me to write a blog and I will be really brave and courageous – provocation and inspiring change on a rare day! Or alternatively, ask me to stand on the edge of a cliff and abseil down I'll be quite cautious and lacking in confidence. We are all a mixture of brave and cautious in different circumstances. School leaders and schools also vary massively, and to those extremes. You may find yourself working with thirty teachers or two hundred; one hundred kids or two thousand five hundred. Either way, decisions always need to be contextualised according to the circumstances in which we work.

Ross Morrison McGill

And then there are Ofsted and Estyn of course. This is what Ross had to say about the current inspection system.

With Ofsted saying around 15 per cent of schools in England are 'Requires Improvement' or 'Inadequate' and with half a million teachers in the system, we are looking at between 40,000 and 50,000 teachers who are living this nightmare every day. Whether they have been pushed into this situation or have chosen to work there, they are working tirelessly in a system, that no matter how courageous the decision making of the leaders, the demographics of the children they have suggests that they will never achieve that elusive 'Outstanding' grade.

Removing Ofsted gradings would be an obvious start. It would solve the recruitment and retention issues overnight. It would also stop this poison, where many school leaders become besotted with Ofsted terminology, e.g. rhetoric such as, 'Our version of Outstanding is better than anyone else's', which I once heard an executive headteacher cite to our staff when a multi-academy trust took over the school. This is what we have created. A system of winners and losers; a structure of we are better than you, despite us all working for the best for every child.

I am all for high standards and accountability. There is a great deal of money in education and as we know, children only get one chance in life, but we do need a more thoughtful approach to how we lead our schools – with high standards.

Somebody brave in our Ofsted or Department for Education (DfE) offices needs to be bold and make a courageous decision for change, at national level, because the difficulty is that people at the highest levels want to keep their jobs too. We all have so many views on what we want from education, that we cannot see that the most obvious solutions for the system are right in front of us. We need to unpick the way we measure and test students, ask ourselves 'why' and then seek 'how' we approach the future; as well as determine the success of a school – and on a level playing field.

Someone must make that leap of faith. This could be someone at the very helm, or it could be thousands of school leaders who make a stand collectively. We only need to turn to social media to see headteacher bloggers cited in Ofsted and DfE speeches. We are being heard, but we all need to do it and we need to make a start.

Ross Morrison McGill

I agree with Ross that the system needs reworking, but how can a school leader be more courageous when faced with an imminent Ofsted inspection? For me, it is as Patrick Ottley-O'Connor told me in a conversation for this book: 'It is not about fighting them but learning to dance with them instead.' Politely standing your ground takes courage and courage requires confidence.' There are so many unknowns in the process, so it pays to prepare thoroughly and control the controllables. Try out my top ten tips to build your confidence and therefore your courage for dealing with the inspectors.

Top tips to build your confidence and courage for Ofsted

1. Knowledge is power so understand how you are going to be judged.
2. Keep up with the latest framework and guidance. Take the mystery out of the process.
3. It is a test of how well you know your school, so be clear about what you are good at and what you need to improve upon.

4. Be prepared to talk about any shortcomings your data may show, the actions you have already taken and their impact.
5. You can't know everything, so be ready to draw on other people.
6. Have somebody, a colleague in another school perhaps, whom you can ring during the process and get an outside perspective from.
7. Practise arguing your position. Find a colleague to act as devil's advocate.
8. Have a clear written plan of what should happen when the call comes (see Chapter 10 (p. 161) for an example of this).
9. Ensure all staff are well briefed and know your identified areas for improvement and what steps are being taken.
10. Remember, you know your school. Be brave and show it to them.

School leaders, on the whole, are a self-deprecating bunch of people. They don't tend to talk about the challenges they have faced to other people, nor the courage they needed to overcome them. It is probably modesty or perhaps the desire not to put others off from applying for leadership roles in the future. The result of not discussing courage as an important trait for any school leader is that we run the risk of leaving people unprepared. Even eight years serving as a deputy did not prepare me for the feelings I experienced when, in my first term as a headteacher, I had to permanently exclude a child.

Those seeking to become the next generation of school leaders should do so under no illusions; they are going to need courage and in some measure. Perhaps if we discussed courage in leadership to a greater degree, it would inspire more people to apply for leadership positions in schools, rather than less, and better prepare them for the challenges of the job.

Effective school leaders are not fearless, but they do demonstrate courage

Here is how they demonstrate courage:

- **They know their school data** – They face facts and if they have have been in post for some time, they avoid looking at things through rose-tinted spectacles. Only by knowing the true state of your department or school can you lead other people forward.

- **They talk straight** – This can feel awkward and uncomfortable at times, especially if conflict is involved. They are respectful and polite. Diplomacy has a place of course but courageous leaders have those crucial conversations. Clarity of expectations helps cut through the smoke and move the issue forwards. They have the courage to make their opinions known even if they know they are going to be unpopular.
- **They hold themselves accountable** – They expect people to perform and deliver on their commitments, and have the courage to challenge them if they don't follow through on them. They accept that accountability begins with them and they model the behaviours they expect to see in others.
- **They address performance issues** – Confronting people is one of the hardest parts of the job, particularly if you like them! Courageous leaders don't fall into the trap of ignoring them and hoping that things will improve. They rarely do! Ignore them and they become toxic, affecting morale and the general performance of the team. Courageous leadership nurtures and encourages, but sometimes it is about grasping the nettle and confronting poor teaching. By taking swift action, they are doing everyone a favour. With willingness and proper, structured support, many (though not all) performance issues can be turned around. For some though, teaching will just not be the right job and they may need an exit strategy that allows them to leave with their dignity intact.
- **They ask for feedback (and listen!)** – None of us are perfect as leaders. We all have blind spots that can potentially impact on our effectiveness. Unfiltered 360-degree feedback is not always easy to hear, but it can prevent us from missing something important.
- **They encourage contributions** – Many leaders feel pressure to have all the answers. You can't, and never will, have *all* the answers. By openly accepting this fact, you are likely to earn respect and encourage healthy debate, and you reinforce the strength of the team and demonstrate that whilst you may not have all the answers, collectively you do. Building trust and relationships and involving staff in decision making builds 'credits in your account' and will make it easier for them to accept bad news and the tough decisions that sometimes need to be made.
- **They communicate clearly and often** – They always try to keep the lines of communication open. It takes courage to refuse to hide behind jargon and fancy technical vocabulary. They talk straight and aren't afraid to say, 'I don't know.' Within the bounds of confidentiality, they share information and keep people in the loop. In the absence of information, people will always make up

their own reality! For example, if you send a message around saying there will be an unscheduled staff meeting at lunchtime but don't say why, people will automatically fill the void of information and probably assume that you are about to be inspected!

- **They help people buy into the vision** – They recognise that people need to feel consulted and listened to. It is no good having a vision if no one else buys into it. It is no good 'leading the charge and going over the top' only to look over your shoulder and find that everyone else is still 'back in the trench'. You will not last long! They recognise the need to bring staff along in the change process for them to truly engage.
- **They give the credit to others** – Strong leaders don't feel the need for constant praise and being in the spotlight themselves and have the courage to give the credit to those around them instead. It can feel a little scary at first. You can start to ask yourself the question, 'Will I be considered irrelevant or unnecessary if other staff seem to be doing all the good stuff?' It takes courage and a parking of egos, but as the quote says:

A good leader takes a little more than his [or her] share of the blame, a little less than his [or her] share of the credit.

Arnold H. Glasow

All school leaders are courageous to some degree, otherwise they would not put themselves through the application process and risk the potential humiliation of rejection. Nobody likes to be rejected. However, some leaders are more courageous in their decision making and leadership style than others and all of us, as Ross Morrison McGill noted above, can feel quite courageous in some situations and less so in others.

My first deputy head, Richard Gerver, was always something of a maverick and a risk-taker. It was and is in his nature. He went on to become the head of a large primary that had poor results and had seen a succession of leaders. His innovative approaches saw a rapid change in the school's fortunes. He would argue that, as Yazz and the Plastic Population once sang, 'The only way is up', and in some ways that made it easier to be innovative, because just doing more of the same thing really wasn't an option. Nonetheless, it took courage to break with conventional approaches and take on the sceptics.

Other leaders find that courage comes from experience. Julie has been a headteacher for six years now. She told me recently that when she was first in post she felt obliged to answer every email that came from her local authority (usually requesting information and statistics) that same day, and ended up running around like a headless chicken all day in order to gather the information needed, only to never hear of the matter again. As time went by and she gained in confidence, she came to realise that one way of sifting and prioritising what was really important was to sit on the emails for a few days. In some cases she would never hear of the matter again, but if she got a follow-up email chasing for the information, then she knew it was something that was really important, rather than emails for emails' sake (the bane of every busy school leader's life!). Again, it takes courage.

So, if courage is partly a product of our nature but also of our experiences, it is natural that school leaders will possess it in different measures. Some will be risk-takers and others will be more cautious by nature. We are all different but I suspect, deep down, that most of us would like to feel a little more courageous at times than we actually do.

> *A ship in harbour is safe – but that is not what ships are built for.*
>
> John A. Shedd

But can you build and develop courage as a leader?

Yes – I believe you can.

I wish I could say that I'm a fearless person, but I'm not. At best, I'm a person who does some frightening things even though I may be terrified whilst doing them. I have never done anything like skydiving (I don't like flying at the best of times; it takes all my courage to get on a plane – why on earth would I then want to throw myself out of it?). The most courageous thing I have done in recent years is give the opening keynote at the NAHT conference at the Liverpool Arena and Conference Centre. I was being followed by the Shadow Education spokesperson. The auditorium was huge and so was the stage, complete with a massive video screen behind me. I felt more nervous than I had done about anything in a very long time, but thankfully my speech was well received, and I learned a lot from it.

So let's look at some steps we could take to grow our courage as school leaders in situations we feel less confident about.

1. Be specific about your fears

Identifying the specific fears you are grappling with enables you to understand them and build the courage to deal with them.

In the case of the NAHT keynote, my fears were:

- Freezing under the lights and forgetting what it was I was going to say.
- Stammering – I developed a pronounced stammer ten years ago when I was suffering from stress-related anxiety. I have largely mastered it, but it does occasionally rear its head when I am under pressure.

Time to reflect

Write a list of your fears both professionally and personally. This may help you to develop a plan to overcome them and build your courage. This is not an easy thing to do, but don't feel embarrassed or ashamed – we all have them. Fear can be a woolly thing so writing specific concerns and worries down gives clarity to them.

1 Professional

2 Personal

Once I had identified my fears of presenting at the NAHT conference, I took a number of steps to deal with them:

- I arrived at the conference centre very early; there is nothing worse than being stuck in traffic and wondering if you will make it on time.
- I spent some quiet time just sitting at the back of the auditorium, watching the AV team set up. It is difficult for the body to remain in a heightened state of anxiety for long periods, so if you can spend some time in the space in which you need to find courage it helps.
- I shared my fears with the AV team. They were brilliant and whilst they set up, they let me practise on stage, so that I could visualise what it would be like, using the space and looking out into the auditorium rather than looking at it from the audience's viewpoint. They even let me practise with the timer.

Once I had done all this, I was well on the way to managing my fears. Note that I say 'managing' rather than 'conquering'. I was still nervous but I could now picture what it would be like to successfully deliver the speech.

2. Use visualistion

Put simply, visualisation is the use of pictures or mental imagery of a desired outcome to an event and how we can make it happen. It can help us to better control our emotions and achieve focus.

How does it work?

When you imagine yourself performing an action perfectly and doing exactly what you want to do, you physiologically create neural patterns in your brain, just as though you had actually physically performed the action. The thought can stimulate our nervous system in the same way that the event would do.

Performing or rehearsing an event in the mind trains the neural patterns to teach our muscles exactly what we want them to do. The more we practise, the stronger those patterns become, increasing the likelihood of a successful outcome when we meet the situation for real.

Visualisation is a technique used by many successful athletes. Watch tennis players rehearse their serve in their head whilst bouncing the ball prior to service, or a rugby player looking from the ball to the posts several times before kicking the ball over the cross bar and between the posts for a conversion.

I run movies inside my head of me being successful in the situation that demands courage from me. It helps boost my levels of self-confidence when I am nervous. If I was worried about a difficult meeting with a parent, I knew I could not accurately visualise the whole meeting; there would be too many variables. However, I would visualise where I would have people sitting and what my opening lines might be. Rehearsing that made me more confident and I knew that if I could get the opening minutes of the meeting right, then I stood a much better chance of the rest of the meeting going well.

3. Go outside your comfort zone

Speaking at that conference took me quite a way out of my comfort zone. Managing my fears gave me the courage to tackle something daunting and gave me a huge boost in confidence. My comfort zone expanded, giving me the courage to tackle other challenges. I recently delivered a whole-day input on resilience to a group of NHS consultant psychologists; it was on resilience and stress management. It was a real challenge. They were a lovely group to work with, but boy, was it intense! I felt like my head was made of glass and that they could all see the innermost workings of my brain! (Not much going on in there most of the time, to be fair!) Again, this too has built confidence and courage. The author Paul McGee (2012) once suggested that if we don't step outside our comfort zone, that zone does not remain the same size; it actually starts to shrink and we become comfortable with less and less. Believe me, I know. Ten years ago, when I was unwell, it took all my courage just to leave the house.

4. Recognise your own courage as a leader

As I have already suggested, listing your fears is an important first step in developing the courage to manage them. However, you should also recognise that you already display courage in many situations. Everyone has courage, whether it is recognised by others or hidden. For example, the very act of applying for a new job, with all that that entails, demands great courage.

Time to reflect

Give yourself the credit you deserve and list five occasions when you have displayed courage in your leadership.

1

2

3

4

5

5. Avoid comparing yourself to others

We are all different and comparing yourself to other people can lower your self-confidence.

I can remember the interview process for my second headship, the largest primary school in our local authority. It was to be a two-day process and there were six candidates in total. I was probably the youngest and least experienced. I knew a couple of the other candidates slightly, but there was one man from a different area altogether. We will call him Mr X. Throughout the first morning, whenever we were not actively engaged in school council interviews or 'in-tray exercises', we would be sat in the staffroom with the other candidates. Mr X was very vocal. It appeared that there was very little he had not done and he clearly believed himself to have superpowers of some description. When I thought of what I had achieved by comparison, I felt my confidence ebbing away. I knew that if I was to stand any remaining chance in the process, I had to get away from Mr X. I had quite a time to wait until my next task so I eventually plucked up the courage to walk down the corridor and ask the office manager if there was anything I could do to help in the office whilst I waited. Within minutes I was stuffing letters in envelopes ready to go out to parents. They were playing Norah Jones' *Come Away With Me* in the background. I felt useful and began to recover my spirits.

It turns out that stuffing envelopes was kryptonite to Mr X's Superman. He was the first candidate to be sent home and only lasted to the end of the first morning! No one likes a smart alec.

We all do it sometimes, but avoid comparing yourself to other people. Focusing on yourself is essential to building your confidence and courage.

6. Look for the positive and avoid the negative

Negative thoughts and attitudes can chip away at your confidence and courage. Part of my cognitive behaviour therapy in my recovery after my breakdown involved regularly writing down things that I was worrying about or that were making me anxious in one column of a piece of A4 paper, and then challenging myself to look for the positive in the situation by answering the question, 'What's another way of looking at this?' Sometimes we might need the help of a trusted friend or colleague to be able to achieve this, but seeking out the positive in any situation will help build your overall courage.

7. Keep moving forward

We all have negative thoughts, which is normal and acceptable. We are wired up to think negatively – it is part of our self-preservation instinct – but try not to dwell on negativity. Take action. Do something positive that will improve your situation. By always moving towards the positive, you will be able to change your negative attitude.

8. Remember fear itself can harm you

Our brain is programmed to experience fear in order to keep us safe. However, it can be dangerous to us. I don't just mean in the sense that stress and anxiety can seriously damage your physical and mental health (they can!), but fear can affect us in more immediate ways too. It can prevent us from applying for a promotion to a post that we are perfectly capable of performing well in, or it can stop us from trying an activity that may well enrich our lives (not skydiving!). It can also affect us in other high-pressure situations, such as freezing in a presentation to colleagues or parents. I knew of one headship candidate who had done the rounds at interview but would pass out under the pressure of the situation. On one occasion, he passed out, hit his head on the corner of a desk and had to be taken to hospital. Needless to say, he didn't get the job. Poor bloke!

Knowing that fear has the potential to harm you can help you set it to one side and concentrate on the immediate challenge.

9. Remember that fear is largely about chemicals

We might think that it is our sense of judgment deciding whether something is dangerous to us and whether we should be afraid, but what actually happens is that fear chemicals flood our brains. Experiments have proven that fear can be induced artificially by injecting these chemicals (Bremner, 2014). We don't want to completely ignore these chemicals but nor do we want them to rule the roost. As Paul McGee would put it, we need to give our rational brains a chance! When we do that, we are more likely to show the courageous leadership that we know, deep down, we are capable of.

Summary

- Courageous school leadership is not about the absence of fear but about acting even when you are afraid and when you know what is the right thing to do.
- Staying in the known may be more comfortable, but comfort zones shrink if we do not step outside them.
- School leaders will need to demonstrate courage in their day-to-day interactions.
- Sometimes it takes courage to stand out from what other schools may be doing.
- Know your school and be realistic about its situation.
- Talk straight and hold others (and yourself) to account.
- Communicate clearly and help others to buy into the vision.

- Give credit where it is due.
- Write your fears down.
- Run positive movies in your head.
- Recognise your own courage as a leader.

---

5 Decisiveness

Decisiveness is a characteristic of high-performing men and women. Almost any decision is better than no decision at all.

Brian Tracy (2004)

Now we turn to our fifth balloon of resilience: decisiveness. The best school leaders make sound, defensible decisions in a timely fashion, especially in times of crisis and uncertainty. Simply put, a decisive leader has the ability to make appropriate decisions in a manner that reflects the level of urgency of the situation. Selecting a scheme of work, for example, requires a decision, but it may be appropriate to take several weeks to arrive at a decision. However, other situations, such as an intruder being reported on site, require that decisive action is taken urgently. Decisiveness is a trait that draws heavily on past experience to influence how it is implemented.

As an interim headteacher, Patrick Ottley-O'Connor has faced an eye-watering 21 Ofsted inspections in different schools and, as we will see in Chapter 10 (p. 161), has a well-rehearsed procedure when the call comes. Someone facing their first inspection in the role of head is understandably likely to be less decisive in those initial minutes. You do not want to rush and make the wrong decision but equally you don't want to be paralysed by fear and make no decision at all.

It's…

12.03pm

I arrive, slightly late, at The Hollybrook Inn, in Derby, ready to meet my friend and former deputy head, Richard, for our semi-regular catch-up. Richard, by contrast has arrived slightly early and is already sat at a table having ordered a pint of bitter for me and a sparkling water for himself (he's on a bit of a health drive at the moment!).

12.16pm

We've spent the last few minutes having a general catch-up on where in the world we have been to over the last few weeks and what we have been up to.

Richard says, 'Shall we order some food?'

'Yes, that sounds like a good idea,' I reply and pick up the fold-out menu listing the culinary delights on offer at this hostelry. I sip at my beer as my eyes scan the menu. Uncharacteristically, I am silent and so is he. He is not silent because he is looking at the menu; he has already decided. He is silent because he does not want to disturb me from my decision-making process.

12.21pm

Richard clears his throat.

'What you having then?' he says.

'Not sure yet,' I reply. 'Don't rush me.'

12.24pm

'Well?' he says, 'Have you decided?'

'Nearly.'

12.25pm

'What are you having,' I ask.

'The chicken salad,' he replies, slightly biting his lip.

Blimey! He really is going for it on this health kick. This does not sound like my kind of a pub meal and I make a mental note to dismiss all the items on the menu that are in the box labelled, 'Lighter bites and salads'.

12.27pm

'Right! I have decided,' I pronounce, 'I am going to have the steak and ale pie!'

'At last, a decision! I'll get these,' he generously offers and makes his way towards the bar to place our order.

He's halfway between our table and the bar when I call out, 'Wait!'

He freezes, but does not turn around.

'I think I'll have a cheese and bacon burger.'

He silently shakes his head and continues to the bar to place the order.

12.30pm

He returns, wearily, and as he retakes his seat he mutters under his breath.

'It's always a bloody burger!'

Richard is absolutely right, of course. It is always 'a bloody burger' (and I don't mean in the sense of being undercooked here!) that I end up choosing. I think it is partly habit to be honest. Whenever I am working away from home and stopping in a hotel, a burger is invariably the cheapest item on the restaurant menu. So for all my procrastination, and detailed studying of the menu, a burger it is. I know that Richard does sometimes find my inability to reach a decision a little trying at times, particularly when he knows the inevitable outcome.

I would like to think that as a headteacher, I was fairly decisive, but that tendency to procrastinate certainly showed itself at times. Seven or eight years ago, before the current programme of savage real-term budget cuts took hold, my school had some money to spend on some redecoration. (Oh those were the days!) We had in the region of 27 classrooms by this stage, following the rapid expansion of the school. I am assuming the builders who had decorated the school previously had got a good deal on orange paint, because all of those classroom doors were painted the same 'muted tangerine' colour, in addition to the doors to all offices, halls, the medical room, library and storerooms. Probably 50 or 60 doors in total – all pretty much identical.

For a visually impaired child it made navigating the building independently difficult. It also made directing parents, who were less familiar with the building, on parents' evening difficult.

'Go through the first set of orange doors ahead of you and turn right. Go through a set of double orange doors and Miss Rashid's classroom is the third orange door on the left!'

'Pardon?'

It looked really corporate and more like an office in places. It was not vibrant and individual, although to be fair the teachers had adorned their orange doors with various pieces of artwork to make them look more distinctive.

I knew a very good decorator who was pretty competitive and set about changing things so that no two rooms in a corridor had the same coloured door. This would involve selecting a pallet of six or seven colours to use. Simple!

Not so simple! I was presented with a massive colour chart, which had every colour under the sun (except muted tangerine!). It took me ages to decide, I think partly because I was aware that I would be living with the consequences of my choices for many years to come (and so would everyone else).

The work was of course going to be carried out over the summer holiday. Having finally made my choice of colours, the decorator wanted me to label every door with the colour I wanted it painting. More decisions – aargh!

So, I am aware that my ability to procrastinate could affect my work sometimes. However, in other situations I could be very decisive. For example, I think my instincts about people were generally quite good and I could make a decision about who I thought the successful candidate should be at interview quite quickly. Fortunately, the governors were generally in agreement with me. These too were decisions the consequences of which I (and everybody else in school) would be living with, for many years to come. I got it wrong once or twice, but we also made some great appointments over the years.

Time to reflect

- Can you think of an occasion when, as a leader, you found it difficult to make a decision?

- What do you think were the underlying causes of your indecision?

Why are we so indecisive sometimes?

For many of us, there are likely to be two possible causes for indecision.

1. Lack of information

As a head of department, for example, it is very difficult to make clear decisions about the future direction of the department if you don't know what resources you are being allocated for the next year. As a headteacher, you cannot make clear decisions about school structure until you know your staffing levels and you cannot determine that until you know your budget allocation.

In such situations, the timing of the availability of that information may be beyond your control, but there may also be situations where gathering additional information may help you reach a decision.

For example, in the last couple of years a number of local authorities have withdrawn their staff absence pooled premium insurance schemes. In some instances this has happened at very short notice, catching some schools unaware and leaving heads, bursars and governors somewhat bewildered. A company called 'The Education Broker' broker staff absence insurance deals from different companies and help schools to make like-for-like comparisons. They have run a number of non-biased, regional information sessions for schools in such circumstances, letting them know the options available to them after the LA schemes are withdrawn. I know all this because they kindly booked me as a guest speaker to talk about some of my experiences around the issue of stress and staff absence.

Many people arrived looking perplexed and anxious as they had very little information on which to base a decision on what to do next. By coming along and spending half a day listening and asking questions, they left looking a great deal more relaxed having sought out the relevant information to make decisions back at school.

2. Lack of conviction

The second reason that we sometimes struggle to make a decision is due to a lack of conviction.

In other words, our gut instinct is not giving us a strong lead one way or another. This might be characterised by the choice of staying in your present school or applying for a promotion you have seen in another school 20 miles away. Sure, you can gather more information, by sending off for an application pack or by looking around the school… But what if you are still not sure? Leadership decisions where your gut instinct is not giving you a steer are often the hardest ones to make.

So what can we do to be more decisive?

There is no easy answer to this, as every circumstance is different and so is every decision, but first, try to set yourself clear deadlines by which you will make a choice.

The Law of Proportional Decision Making states that the amount of time spent making a decision should be directly proportional to the significance of its outcome. In other words, big decisions with big outcomes need more time whilst smaller decisions with relatively small outcomes require much less time. For example, the decision whether to move house or not potentially has very significant outcomes (higher rent or mortgage, longer journey to school, etc.), and this is why we take time making it. The decision to leave the house without brushing your hair when you are late has a relatively minor outcome (particularly for me with my receding hairline), so we don't need more than a split second to decide.

The law is logical and simple and we apply it a lot of the time in our day-to-day lives (although I wish I could apply it to choosing from a pub menu!), but do we always apply it in our leadership roles?

An effective school does need to apply their decision making consistently. You can't make irrational decisions sometimes and then be calm and collected on other occasions. Your team will never know what to expect from you or how to approach you from one decision to another and it is our job as leaders to create an environment where everyone can thrive.

Not being able to make decisions about a pub menu has comparatively trivial consequences (apart from keeping Richard waiting), but not being able to make leadership decisions at school can potentially have very serious consequences.

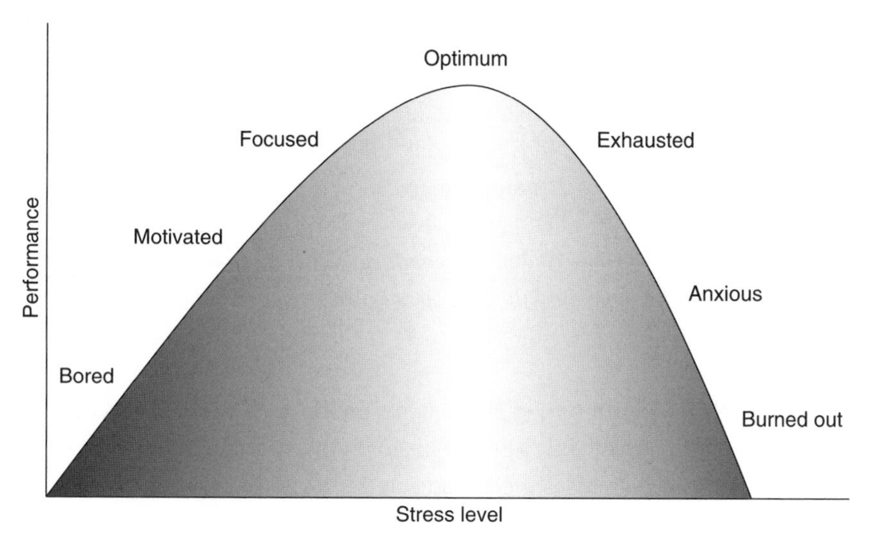

Figure 5.1 The stress performance curve

I believe that there can be a link between procrastination and burnout. We all need some pressure in our lives. As the stress curve above shows, without demands being made of us we can easily become listless, bored and demotivated, which can affect our performance. Pressure can be very motivating and can help fend off procrastination. But once we get beyond the peak of performance, we can quickly slide down into overload, anxiety and burnout. As we approach burnout, we are often exhausted and unable to think clearly and rationally, and we struggle to make decisions, thereby increasing our tendency to procrastinate at this end of the curve too.

In his excellent book *Eat That Frog*, author Brian Tracy reminds us of an old saying that if the first thing you think you have to do each morning is to eat a live frog, then you would at least know that you had probably got the worst thing you were likely to have to do that day out of the way (Tracy, 2004). In other words, when you look at your 'to do list' in the morning, you should get the one thing you would really rather put off out of the way with first!

Certainly, when I was unwell back in 2006 and fast approaching the burnout point that I reached in early 2007, I would put off making decisions about the important things (mostly for fear of making the wrong decisions), such as addressing an underperformance in outcomes in maths, which I did not know how to effectively address. Instead, I expended my time addressing the smaller issues that would have less impact but that made me look busy. For example, I spent a lot of time in site meetings for building projects around school that I probably didn't need to attend.

I am sure that Brian Tracy would describe this as a classic case of the 'Pareto Principle', or the '80/20 Rule' as it is often referred to. Pareto, a nineteenth-century economist, observed that people in society seem to naturally divide things up into the vital 20 per cent of things that would affect income and influence and the 80 per cent of things in life that are more trivial.

> *This means that if you have a list of ten items to do, two of those items will turn out to be worth five or ten times more than the other eight items put together.*
>
> Brian Tracy (2004)

Tracy notes that even supposing all the items on the list may take a similar time to address, most people tend to procrastinate on the 'vital few' that will have the most impact. They then focus their efforts on the 'trivial' 80 per cent, where they will have the least impact.

I will never look at my 'to do list' in quite the same light again!

So what can we do to avoid this? Well, time spent planning is a real investment. The better the plan is the less likely we are to procrastinate.

Paralysis of decision making, combined with poor communication, damages your credibility as a leader and, at worst, can cause blind panic.

I think that anyone taking the time to read this book would recognise that strategic as well as day-to-day decisiveness is one of the most vital success attributes for school leaders at every level, but we all possess it in different quantities.

So, why is it that some people can make strong, bold and quick decisions, whilst at the same time others wobble, procrastinate and apparently delay or avoid just getting on with it?

Well we have already established that experience can play a part in this. If you have faced a leadership challenge before and dealt with it successfully, it will give you some confidence in your approach. If you were not so successful, it will at least give you some pointers in terms of what not to do second time around.

American author Nick Tasler argues that there are, however, other elements at play (Tasler, 2014). Two of them particularly struck a chord with me in terms of school leadership: being decisive by nature and being decisive by training.

Being decisive by nature

In a study conducted at the University of Michigan, psychologist Georges Potworowski discovered that certain personality traits such as emotional stability, self-efficacy and self-confidence predict why some people are naturally more decisive than others (Potworowski, 2010).

When facing a decision based on two strategic options of comparable merit, timid and less emotionally stable leaders will tend to fear upsetting anyone, says Tasler (Tasler, 2014). Such school leaders will let debates drag on in meetings for weeks or even months before selecting a grotesque 'Frankenstein's monster' of a solution pieced together, which actually ends up pleasing no one but which both sides can merely tolerate. The team goes on to make a moderate amount of progress on a moderate number of objectives. The team successfully achieves complete mediocrity and so does their leader!

By contrast, more decisive school leaders will welcome contributions from their team as they recognise that they themselves cannot have all the answers. However, they will make it clear from the outset that whilst they will carefully consider both sides of any argument and welcome healthy debate, they will ultimately choose the course of action that they judge to be the best for their pupils and the school. They make the decision without procrastination and move promptly to enlist the help of both sides in executing the decision. Some staff inevitably will not be thrilled with the choice but are still (quietly!) pleased to finally have a decision and some clarity of direction. The team makes more significant progress, I suspect, in the chosen strategic direction of travel, which should be reflected in improved outcomes.

Being decisive by training

In the 1990s, Shelley Taylor of the University of California, Los Angeles and Peter Gollwitzer of the University of New York discovered that when we are considering a decision that we have not yet made, almost all people exhibit the same personality traits, such as neuroticism, a loss of sense of control and pessimism (Taylor and Gollwitzer, 1995). These were all traits that Potworowski 's study at Michigan (see above) had linked to indecisiveness. However, these are temporary states. The researchers found that, as soon as we make a decision and start planning the steps for executing it, our brains automatically switch gears. Suddenly we feel more confident and in control.

This is the perfect mindset for acting more decisively.

In other words, we all have the potential within us to be decisive or indecisive. In any one day, we might slip in and out of this decisive mindset. Nick Tasler argues that excellent leaders have learned how to make 'decisive' their default setting. The ability to make that leap of decisiveness places them in a more decisive mindset, which leads to even more decisiveness and so on (Tasler, 2014).

There is no magic wand to be waved that will develop the ability to be decisive. It is a mindset – a mental attitude that comes out of practice and persistence.

Before you can be decisive, you need some clarity of thinking to fully understand the challenge and your situation. This is sometimes easier said than done in the pressured world of school leadership.

The following are techniques that I have found useful in gaining clarity of mind.

Clarity

1. **Believe in yourself** – Tell yourself that you are a decisive person. Quit telling yourself and other people that you are indecisive (I know I have just told you!). It's a good story but actually it doesn't help you much if you really want to make quick, firm decisions.
2. **There are no bad decisions** – Have faith that no matter which decision you choose, there is always a lesson behind it, and that you will benefit from it, regardless of the outcome. The only bad decisions are the ones we do not learn anything from. Action is better than inaction.
3. **Be brave** – Don't be afraid to make 'mistakes'. Over time we get better at evaluating situations, information and our emotions.
4. **Instincts** – Listen to your instincts. Trust your gut feelings – they are usually right. Pay attention to what your inner voice is saying to you.
5. **Write things down** – Clearly define the question to be answered and underneath write down your options as well as any other thoughts or concerns you may have. Just dump all your thoughts to the paper as they enter your mind. Don't edit, just write it all down. Don't worry if your thoughts do not flow to begin with; if you keep going things will become clearer.
6. **Take a step back** – Even if you only see a limited set of options, there will be others. Try to share with someone outside the immediate situation and creatively brainstorm alternative solutions.
7. **Set yourself a time limit** – Give yourself a clear deadline to make the decision. We often don't actually need a lot of time to make sound decisions, we just think we do and it can become a habit.

Decisive leadership

In order to be an effective and decisive leader, it is important that you have self-confidence and work at building the confidence of your team. Having confidence in yourself and knowing that you have the confidence of the people you lead enables you to act more easily, think more clearly and put your team at ease.

Time to reflect

Remind yourself of three occasions when you demonstrated decisive leadership. What were the circumstances? How did other people react? How did you feel?

1

2

3

So, accepting that our leadership decisiveness skills are partly down to our previous experiences, our nature and our training, what can we do to develop the parts of those skills that are within our control?

Demonstrate competence

Firstly, you need to demonstrate yourself to be competent. That does not mean that you need to know everything, but you do need to 'know your stuff'. Without that, people may like you but they will not necessarily trust you. If staff trust you, they are more likely to support your judgements and do what needs to be done once a decision is made.

Have a clear long-term vision

You need a clear long-term vision of what you want to achieve in the school, department or subject you lead. Some decisions need to be taken quickly, but this is one you need to spend time over because if you have a clear vision, the smaller day-to-day decisions are much easier to take as they become steps towards those long-term goals.

Asking yourself the question 'By doing this, will it move us nearer to our long-term goal?' can bring clarity to the decision-making process. Remind yourself of your 'Why?' – your sense of purpose. Does the decision you are contemplating align with your 'Why?'? If not, you are moving further away from what you set out to achieve.

Map out your 'What?', 'Why?' and 'How?'. It is far easier to arrive at a decision when you are completely clear on what it is you are trying to achieve, why you are trying to achieve it and how you plan on achieving it.

Time invested in planning can save time making decisions in the longer term.

Break decisions down into smaller components

By breaking down big decisions into several smaller decisions it gives you as a leader the opportunity to test, evaluate and modify your plan if things don't work out. Breaking decisions down reduces the risk, meaning that there is less riding on any one individual decision. This in turn allows us to make decisions with a greater degree of confidence.

Gather information

You need to be able to make an informed decision. Gather as much information relevant to the decision as you possibly can. You don't have to do all that yourself. Successful and resilient leaders delegate and make use of the strengths of the team they lead.

You must be able to distinguish between 'facts' that have been carefully tested and those that have been just been asserted or assumed.

Remember, it is not a perfect world and leaders everywhere often have to make decisions based on incomplete information. Set yourself a clear deadline for making a decision. Don't let things drag on. You can delay and delay and still never receive all the information you expect or hope for. Any decision is better than no decision, even if you then have to alter course.

Seek contributions from others

You cannot know everything and have all the answers, so it is often wise to seek outside input into your decision making, be that other members of a leadership team, a governor or somebody outside of school altogether (within the bounds of confidentiality of course).

> *Truth springs from arguments amongst friends.*
>
> David Hume

If you have fostered a culture of trust and a spirit of collaborative problem-solving, then bringing other people into the decision-making process can bring fresh insights and alternative perspectives, which may shape the final decision. I have lost count of the number of times that another member of our senior leadership team pointed out a key fact that I had actually overlooked. Share information with the participants honestly and openly. It is usually best to do so in a raw form to allow others to draw their own conclusions. If you share it selectively it creates the impression that you already have a position and that you are just going through the motions! Make sure that everyone understands that yours will be the final say but that you genuinely value all their opinions and input. To work, the process relies on trusting and respectful relationships. Without this, the process is likely to develop into a contest between different views, rather than a group effort to test and evaluate alternatives. All too quickly that can lead into a test of strength, the loudest voices are heard, innovative ideas are suppressed, and participants feel that they have to go along with the dominant view to avoid further conflict. Avoid dominating the discussion yourself; it is an easy trap to fall into, particularly for someone like me who rather likes the sound of my own voice at times!

Consider the alternatives (honestly!)

I can remember when I was head of Key Stage 2 in a school, sitting through a meeting discussing class arrangements for the following year. It was pretty clear to me that our head was glazing over and had actually decided what pattern of organisation he was going for before the meeting had even begun. As I left his office I thought, 'That was a pointless exercise. What a waste of everyone's time'. When I was an inexperienced deputy head I did, to my shame, occasionally act that way so that I could say that I had listened to other people's views before reaching my decision.

Pointless meetings waste not only your precious time, but also that of your entire team.

When leaders consider a number of alternatives, they engage in a deeper, more thoughtful analysis and avoid settling too early on the most obvious answers to the problem. However, just giving other people the opportunity to air their views is not enough. If they feel their voice was never properly heard or actually honestly considered, this leads to resentment and ultimately resistance to the final decision. Whilst not every participant can 'come out on top' in the process, it is vital that the leaders make it absolutely clear to other participants that they had a genuine opportunity to influence the outcome. You have to convey openness and honesty by actively listening and, where appropriate, investigating the alternative ideas presented further before arriving at your decision

Analyse the risks

Ask yourself, 'What are the risks attached with making this decision?', 'What's the worst that can happen?' and 'What's my desired outcome?' Having done all that, make a decision and sink or swim with the ship. You're a leader and nobody wants one that is perceived to be wishy-washy.

Make a clear yes or no decision and thoroughly explain it to yourself

Making the decision is completely pointless if no action results. In order to give credibility to your decision you need to put it into practice. You need to mobilise the people who need to make things happen and ensure that they have the resources needed to put your decision into practice. Whilst I am not suggesting for one moment that school leaders need to explain every decision that they make, you should be prepared to explain the more strategic ones if you want people to get on board – decisions are so much easier to implement if people are on board! You must explain the thought process behind the call and the options that were discussed and considered. People process messages differently, so try to be concise and avoid ambiguity in what you are saying.

Stay involved

Even if a decision that was made was the correct one at the time, if it is poorly executed it is likely to end up being a poor decision, regardless of how much thought went into it. Decisive school leaders don't simply fire the starting pistol and move on to something else. Rather they stay engaged with the execution and they regularly ask for updates and feedback on the results. If things are not going according to plan, they will make adjustments rather than ploughing on regardless. They will not micromanage people, directing their every turn, but they will provide active support to those involved in carrying the decision out.

> *Set the vision and determine the goals, but trust people to make it happen. Tolerance is good; indecisiveness is bad.*
>
> Stephen Archer (2016)

Make decisions and move forward

If your school is experiencing difficult times, there is likely to be fear and intense change. Decisions need to be made but there is often a fear of making the wrong decision and there is a risk of ending up in lengthy meetings in the style of the BBC comedy programme *W1A*, where nothing ever gets decided. Try to avoid 'analysis paralysis' and make the decision. Forward movement is always better than being stuck in one place. Approach it with determination and an open mind, knowing that it will be messy and that a mid-course correction may be necessary.

The dangers of taking too long to reach a decision are obvious. That having been said, leaders must also consider the dangers of reaching a decision too quickly. Leaders who usually make good decisions recognise that it happens as a result of a process, not at a single point in time.

Summary

- **Decisive leaders make sound, defensible decisions in a timely fashion, especially in times of crisis and uncertainty.**
- **Decisiveness is a trait that draws heavily on past experience.**
- **A lack of information and a lack of conviction can both contribute to indecision.**

- The amount of time spent making a decision should be directly proportional to the significance of its outcome.
- An effective school leader needs to apply their decision making consistently.
- Most people spend most of their energy and time on the trivial 80 per cent and procrastinate about the vital ten per cent.
- Some people are decisive by nature, some by training or, more realistically, a combination of the two.
- Resilient and decisive leaders:
  - demonstrate their competence, building trust
  - have a clear long-term vision of where they want to get to
  - break decisions down into smaller components
  - gather information to inform decisions
  - seek contributions from others
  - consider the alternatives
  - analyse the risks
  - stay involved.

---

6 Asking for help

Do not be afraid to ask for help. Nobody gets through college on their own.
Michelle Obama

And so on to the sixth balloon: a willingness to ask for help. When many of us think of successful leaders in all walks of society, as well as thinking of them as being courageous and decisive, we often imagine them to be self-reliant; they are an island, needing no one.

'What do you mean by self-reliance?' I hear you say.

Self-reliance means being emotionally self-sufficient.

Self-reliant school leaders are self-motivated. They lead. They are not dependent on others to provide them with motivation; rather they are the source of their own motivation. They also do not need the approval of other people, or to be 'psyched up' by others. The source of a leader's motivation and self-esteem comes from within. Psychologists describe these kinds of people as having an internal locus of control. In other words, they find their primary motivation from within themselves.

People who are not self-reliant need to be motivated by external influences. This could be their headteacher, or chair of governors (if they are a head), partner or the need to earn money to feed their kids and keep a roof over their head. If this kind of external motivating force is not there then the individual becomes demotivated, lethargic and perhaps even fearful.

Time to reflect

- To what degree would you say have an internal locus of control?
- Are you a self-motivated individual?
- To what extent do you generate your own motivation from the inside out?
- What external influences also motivate you?

Self-reliant school leaders do not need or seek the approval of others. Nor do they fear the disapproval of others. Realistically, everyone fears the disapproval of others to some degree (I have never met a head yet who shows no concern about what criticisms inspectors might level at their school in a report that then goes out to parents), but non-self-reliant people do not take criticism well. A lesson observation that went badly, for example, will smart for some time to come. I know myself that if I am speaking at a conference and receive 99 positive evaluations and one negative one, it will be the negative one that will rankle and stick with me. Some non-self-reliant people are afraid to state their opinion, for fear of being rejected. They get upset and annoyed whenever anyone criticises them or contradicts their views. The fear of disapproval and criticism is sometimes called 'the fear of failure' and 'the fear of rejection'.

Self-sufficient school leaders are less prone to the fear of failure; rather they fear *not* trying to succeed. They are not psyched out by criticism and rejection but recognise that often massive amounts of failure and rejection are necessary precursors to an ultimate success. As Thomas Edison once said in relation to inventing the electric light bulb:

> *I have not failed. I've just found 10,000 ways that won't work.*
>
> Thomas Edison

So, self-sufficient school leaders aren't dispirited by failure, nor by the criticism of others.

Time to reflect

- To what degree would you say you are oversensitive to criticism, rejection and failure?
- If someone criticises your performance, do you become angry, get upset or dispirited?
- Or, do you regard criticism, rejection or failure as *feedback information,* which needs to be analysed and then used to build improved plans for the future?

In many ways, being a self-reliant leader is a very attractive proposition and perhaps you would like to be more self-reliant than you are. Here are my tips on being more self-reliant:

Tips on being more self-reliant

1. Be the source of your own self-confidence. Regularly list and remind yourself of your successes.
2. Don't become reliant on others to motivate you or praise you.
3. Toughen up (a little). We sometimes need to grow a thicker skin.
4. Don't be oversensitive to criticism, particularly if someone is trying to help you improve.
5. Don't allow fear of rejection or failure to haunt you.
6. Remind yourself that usually massive rejection and failure are necessary precursors to success.
7. Treat failure and rejection as feedback information. Analyse it and then use it to build improved plans for a better future.

Asking for help as a school leader

Self-reliant leadership as a notion has a lot going for it, but I do wonder sometimes if we become over-schooled in the idea of independence. It will not always be obvious to other people, or even to ourselves, because self-reliance has become synonymous with words such as 'successful', 'dependable' and 'effective'. However, the acid test of whether you have adopted this approach to your leadership in school is to ask yourself the following question:

How easy do you find it to ask other people for help?

If the answer to this question is 'Not very', then the chances are you are a fairly self-reliant leader.

However, when I ask people what they most like about their school, they rarely mention the building or the parking arrangements. Nor do they mention the data-tracking system or the online risk-assessment programme. They mention one thing: people.

They usually talk first about the kids – the funny things that they come out with and the satisfaction of seeing their faces light up when the penny drops and they finally 'get it'. They then usually talk about their colleagues – the staffroom banter, the sense of camaraderie and being part of a team. It is one of the most rewarding parts of what can be a very pressurised job. I visit many schools in my work and some just seem to have a natural energy to them and it's often born out of that sense of belonging and teamwork. It can take years to develop and, as headteacher, it was one of the things I valued most and was wary of losing as our school rapidly expanded. Why on earth would any leader not want to have that kind culture in their school? It is better for the staff and improves the children's learning too.

happy staff = happy students = happy school

But an aversion to asking for help, namely being overly self-reliant, actually has the *opposite* effect. It causes isolation, separation and fragmentation, the very things that leaders would want to avoid in their school or department.

You see, by asking for help we create a situation where other people feel valued and secure in their position. It raises their self-esteem and we form a connection – an experience shared and not forgotten. The act of doing something for someone else actually makes us feel good and releases endorphins in our brains. Happiness expert Dr Andy Cope (whom I have known and worked with for years, and who kindly wrote the introduction to the book you are now holding!) talks a lot about the positive powerful effects of random acts of kindness, and I agree with him.

Only the other day, I was walking across the pedestrian crossing towards our local Tesco (other supermarkets are available but this one is only a minute away from my house so I'm hardly going to go to any of those, excellent though I am sure they are!) when a woman in her mid-twenties began crossing in the opposite direction towards me. She was pushing a pushchair with one hand and had a very full bag of shopping in the other. (I should point out here that there was a toddler in the pushchair – she wasn't just pushing a pushchair!) As we passed on the crossing, a four-pint plastic bottle of milk fell out of her bag. She had her hands full; I was there so I picked it up for her. She thanked me, we exchanged a smile and went our separate ways. I felt good and hopefully, she did too. A small act of kindness actually set me up for the day.

It's a win–win situation.

Whilst asking for help undoubtedly makes others feel valued and good about themselves, there are many other benefits too.

You may well discover strengths, knowledge and abilities in other people that you may not have noticed in the past. You gain from them different and varying insights. We get into habits of thinking that are sometimes hard to break. Same old thinking, same old problem. Potentially somebody else may completely flip the way you look at a problem and help create a solution that you had not even thought of, let alone considered.

You also start to develop a stronger, trusting and more balanced team that can collectively find answers to a wide range of challenges. As Kim Johnson used to tell his staff in school, 'I don't have all the answers but collectively *we* do!' Good leaders are always seeking to build the people around them. Asking other members of your team for help demonstrates that you value their support, trust in their advice and believe in their competence in their own role.

Comfort zones are, as the name suggests, comfortable, but stay inside them and they do not stay the same size. As we saw in Chapter 4 (p. 78), they actually start to shrink. If you are in a position where you need to ask for help, you are most likely in a situation that is outside of your comfort zone and that's a good thing because, as leader, that's how you grow and develop. Asking for help will mean that you are not facing the situation on your own.

Sometimes school leaders fall into the trap of doing too much for the people they lead. Let's say you have given a deadline to members of staff for handing in some information that you need.

There's a knock on your door. It's Hugh. Hugh asks you for a 48-hour extension on the given deadline and gives a credible reason of some domestic crisis at home. Being the compassionate leader that you are, you say, 'Yes'. Hugh is very grateful and goes on his way. A compassionate thing to have done, the warm glow you feel inside outweighs the minor inconvenience of not receiving the information you requested.

But this can be a slippery slope.

Leadership consultant Dan Miller (2010) puts it something like this:

- When you do something for one of your team for the first time, you create **Appreciation.**
- The second time, you create **Anticipation.**
- The third time, you create **Expectation.**
- The fourth time, you create **Entitlement.**
- The fifth time, you create **Dependency.**

By not asking for help from others but letting them come to us for help, we can actually and unwittingly create a culture of dependence where everyone looks to their leader to find all their solutions, making leaders feel more isolated and under pressure. Leaders who ask for help enable people to do more of what they do best. In other words, staff members can spend more of the time playing to their strengths, which makes them happier and more fulfilled.

Another good reason for asking for help from other members of your team is that you demonstrate to staff that you do not think that you are perfect (they know you aren't!). By asking for help, you are showing that you are a confident leader, not an arrogant one. A little humility is always appreciated.

The important reason for asking for help though, is this:

You are protecting your biggest asset and that is you!

Remember Al Siebert's analogy with the rubber band, discussed in the Introduction (p. 4). It is a useful analogy here too:

- If the band (i.e. you!) is not stretched, then it is not fulfilling its purpose. Bands are designed to be stretched.
- Stretch the band for a time and it will snap back into place when the pressure on it is released.
- However, stretch the band hard and keep it that way over a long period, then the integrity of the band starts to break down and small holes start to appear.
- Superheat the rubber band and the integrity of the band starts to break down.
- Stretch the band too far and it will snap.

Take on too much and you run the risk of snapping the band. If you know you need help, don't see it as a failing but as a protective measure.

So why is it that some school leaders never seem to ask for help? I am sure that their reasons are varied and complex but, in essence, they boil down to two things.

Some leaders (thankfully few) are so arrogant that they believe that they actually *do* know all the answers. They do not value the contributions of their team very highly so why would they want to seek the help of other people? It is all about them. In my experience, leaders like this are not respected – feared perhaps, but not respected. Theirs are not happy schools.

Some leaders, though, don't ask for help but not because they are arrogant. They *know* they don't have all the answers and they are frightened about other people *finding out* that they don't have all the answers! This is called 'Imposter Syndrome' or 'The Emperor's New Clothes'. They are concerned that other people expect them to be all seeing and all knowing and that revealing gaps in their knowledge or skills will show them as weak and they will be somehow diminished in other people's eyes. It is a hard mask to keep in place.

I do some guest lectures for B.Ed students at Derby University, including one on applying for jobs, so that they understand the process from a school's perspective. One of the first things I always say to them is never lie about your achievements, on paper or at the interview. For sure, we all put a positive spin on things, but never lie; you will always worry that you may be found out and that is very draining!

For leaders who struggle to show vulnerability, the job can be very draining too.

Patrick Ottley O'Connor tells the staff in each of the schools where he is interim head, 'As a leader, I am a positive person and I enjoy having a laugh, but I am not superhuman, I get jaded. So, if you see me jaded, stop and talk to me. Smile at me.'

Fundamentally, we cannot expect staff to be open and willing to ask for help from other people if we are not willing to model the same kind of behaviours ourselves. As I have said before, schools eventually become like their leaders.

The key, as a leader, to being able to ask for help is to be able to recognise the entrenched belief that you should always be self-reliant, know what you are doing and have all the answers! I was recently speaking at a conference in the Midlands; on before me was Dame Alison Peacock, Chief Executive of the Chartered College of Teaching. She suggested we should:

> *Dispense with the myth that we have all got it taped.*
>
> Alison Peacock

How right she is. School leaders sometimes wear self-reliance like a suit of armour, and yes, armour can be useful in protecting ourselves. Asking someone else for help requires taking off that armour (at least for now), and admitting that you are a human being, you are fallible, you make mistakes and, on occasion, you are out of your depth. It requires humility to show your vulnerable side to colleagues, but (provided you are not doing it the whole time) I think they will respect you more for it.

Time to reflect

- As a leader, how often do you ask for help when you are struggling?
- Have you ever tried to go it alone, when you were in over your head?
- What sometimes holds you back from asking for help?
- Think of an occasion when you were struggling and did not ask for help. How do you think other people would have felt if they had known?

I was recently talking to Viv Grant, Director of Integrity Coaching.

We spoke about this tension in being self-sufficient as a leader. Viv was very clear that you cannot perform a leadership role without support and that we need to be talking about the vulnerability of the position. There was something else that she said to me that particularly struck a chord:

> *It's the support that gives you the self-reliance.*
>
> Viv Grant

She is absolutely right of course. Being a self-reliant leader and asking for help are not mutually exclusive behaviours.

Yes, I believe you can be totally self-reliant as a leader, for a period of time, *but*:

1. It can have a damaging effect on the culture of the school over time, as you are modelling isolation.
2. It is not sustainable in the long term. With a shortage of people coming forward to take up leadership positions, people wishing to become leaders tend to do so at a younger age and, with the raising of the age of retirement, many people will be in leadership roles for 25 years plus.

I have interviewed and spoken to many school leaders over the last five years, trying to understand why it is that some stay resilient over time and others, sadly, pack up and leave the profession. I can tell you this: many of them have had long and illustrious careers, but they are not careers that have always gone swimmingly. Most have experienced setbacks, disappointments and some have even had to contend with a serious illness, but the one thing that almost all of them have in common was that they knew when to reach out to someone and ask for help. Even Steve Munby, former Chief Executive of The National College of School Leadership and one of the strongest leaders I have met, had a tough time when he worked in local government and nearly quit before reaching out and accepting support.

My own absence from work ten years ago was partly caused by pride – an unwillingness to accept that I was out of my depth at that time. Rather than reaching out to others who might be able to help and understand, I withdrew into myself. I stopped going to heads' meetings and network events. I stayed in my own silo and avoided the very people that understood the pressures (and rewards!) of leadership and would have been in the best position to help me. Regrettably my story is far from unique.

Lesson learned:

Asking for help is not a weakness but a strength.

So, what's the best way to go about asking for help? Here are my top tips.

How to ask for help

1. **When to ask for help** – Be honest with yourself. Do you have the knowledge, skillset and physical and mental capacity to deal with the issue well? If the answer is no, then you should look for support from outside. You cannot be an expert in everything. School leaders often end up being generalists with expertise in one or two areas but a broad range of moderate expertise and knowledge over a wider range of areas.
2. **Encourage a positive response** – You are more likely to receive a positive response to any requests if you are the kind of leader that generously helps others wherever you reasonably can. If you are able to build a positive reputation as someone who helps others, then other people will then want to help you, even those you haven't directly helped. You have engendered goodwill. However, keep in mind that these things tend to have a rather limited shelf life! A historic reputation for helpfulness will get you nowhere. You must keep that reputation alive by helping other people on a regular basis.
3. **Do your homework** – Try to exhaust all the options and be sure that you do not have the capacity to resolve the issue by yourself. Whilst other people in general are usually flattered to be asked and ready to offer assistance, their time is valuable too.
4. **Don't assume you know *what* people know** – Underestimating the willingness of others to help is a common mistake. The fact is, you never know *what* people know or how they may be able to help you until you ask them!
5. **Allow yourself permission** – Give yourself permission to have the conversation. Trust that what you're trying to achieve has value and importance for the school as a whole and, mostly, the pupils. You need to have faith that the support you need will be provided. Most people will be flattered that you have asked.
6. **Don't beat yourself up about asking** – Remember other people in school will benefit from the support you receive. It will ultimately pay dividends for others!

7 **Consider who to ask** – You need to consider who is likely to be in the best position to assist you. Do you ask one person or ask others to contribute?

8 **Connect** – To begin the conversation, make a personal connection. Go and see them and ask if they can spare you some time for a chat. Absolutely *don't* do it by email! It's a conversation so ask them questions. Try to get a sense of the other person's wellbeing, both professionally and personally.

9 **Know what you want to ask** – It sounds obvious I know, but you need to have some clarity on the issue. Identify the area you need help with and try to think what assistance you need. As a leader, you don't want to get into a conversation and appear indecisive, unsure of what you are asking. If you don't know, then the other person most certainly won't! If you don't feel comfortable asking for help, begin by asking for advice, for example, 'I have this dilemma and I would really value your take on things.'

You may well find that an offer of assistance is forthcoming from that opening request. If not, you have at least paved the way for a more direct approach.

10 **Tell the story** – Let them know what it is that you are grappling with and what you're looking for in seeking their help. Is it advice or something practical (or both) that you are seeking?

11 **Keep an open mind** – It may well be that the other person or people come up with practical ways in which they can assist you that you have not considered.

12 **Ask** – Summon your courage, and ask them for the help you need. Be prepared to allow the other person or people to make the decision about what they can best do to help you. You are very unlikely to receive an outright 'No'. The worst that is likely to happen is that they signpost you to someone else who may be better placed to help.

13 **Be honest** – Be clear and open about why you need to ask them for help. Am I asking for too much? Is there something else you think I ought to be asking for?

14 **Be open-minded** – What someone offers may not be exactly what you asked for. Keep an open mind to what you are being offered. Ultimately, you may discover that there is more value in what is being offered than you at first imagined.

15 **Show appreciation** – Close the conversation with sincere appreciation for their time and any assistance offered.

16 **Offer something back** – During the conversation you may have picked up on something you can do to help them. If not, there is no harm in asking.

Like trust, support is reciprocal: the more you give, the more you get in return.

Drs Dennis and Michelle Reina (2015)

Resilient leaders seek support from a wide range of sources, *not because they are weak but because they are strong* enough to recognise that they need to look after themselves in order to be effective.

Earlier in the chapter, I used the analogy of our resilience being like a rubber band (p. 105). Park that image for a moment and think instead of a stool (the milking variety!).

Your resilience is the seat of the stool. It relies on support from underneath by way of the legs. A one-legged stool is feasible, but it is not very stable for the person sitting on it. The stool will be inclined to wobble and possibly fall. The addition of a second leg may provide a little added stability for the person sitting on it, but it is still a precarious seating arrangement where you are unlikely to feel relaxed sitting on the stool. Adding a third leg makes the stool considerably more stable, but cars have four wheels rather than three for a good reason. You can still topple over!

Cue YouTube video: 'Rolling a Reliant Robin', *Top Gear*, BBC (www.youtube.com/watch?v=QQh56geU0X8&t=187s) – go on, check it out!

Four legs really are necessary to provide a properly stable piece of furniture where a person can sit confidently and concentrate on other things!

So, in the analogy with your resilience as a leader, what do the four legs represent?

1. Support from within the school, e.g. mentors or trusted colleagues.
2. Support from professional networks outside of your immediate environment, e.g. cluster or network meetings where you form trusting relationships with people who understand your job but can offer an external perspective.

3 Family support.

4 Support from your wider social circle.

If, as a leader, you are only getting support in one of these areas you are very vulnerable.

Two or three areas and you stand a better chance of staying aloft, but to give yourself the best chance of remaining resilient, you need support in all four areas.

Time to reflect

- Rank the four legs from one to four in terms of the significance of their contribution to your own resilience, with one being the most significant and four being the least significant.

  1

  2

  3

  4

- Given that support is a two-way street, i.e. we have to give in order to receive, what action(s) could you take to increase support in your weakest area and build your resilience?

Social media

Anyone who knows me well will know that I am not very good with technology. Overnight, Windows 10 has done a major automated update on my laptop. It took ages to boot back up this morning at a time when I was itching to get writing and when it finally did spark back into life it had installed a raft of new features that I don't understand, although I note that I can now pin frequently used websites onto my taskbar, which I guess is quite useful. So technology is not really my thing, but I do use Twitter (@jameshilton300 if you want to follow me) and as such I have to acknowledge that social media is rapidly becoming a fifth leg that you can very usefully attach to your stool of resilience.

The hashtag **#teacher5aday** was started by geography teacher and Deputy Head of Eggars School Martyn Reah, back in 2014. It has seen a huge range of problems and solutions shared by teachers on Twitter. The campaign encourages teachers to focus on their wellbeing and, in particular, five areas in their daily lives. It also includes tips on leadership, reflection and reducing workload.

#teacher5aday has attracted praise from a wide range of people, including the influential Ross Morrison McGill, former secondary deputy head and the man behind the popular @TeacherToolkit Twitter feed.

> *The #teacher5aday campaign reminds all teachers to find balance in their working life and spend more precious time with loved ones. It encouraged me to focus more on my own wellbeing as a teacher.*
>
> Ross Morrison McGill

I have been fortunate enough to be a part of this online community over the last two or three years. Martyn even asked me to contribute a vlog recently (that challenged me greatly from a technical point of view, I can tell you!). But what is really interesting to me is that I see teachers from far-flung parts of the UK responding to requests for ideas and advice. Sometimes the person's identity is clear, sometimes not; it depends on what they have chosen as their handle (I almost sound as if I know what I am talking about!). Some of these people may meet regularly at TeachMeets and the like, but others, because of geography, may never meet face-to-face. There is a vast community of people out there for whom social media has given the opportunity to reach out and support one another. It is powerful stuff!

Summary

- Self-reliant school leaders have an internal locus of control.
- They do not need or seek the approval of others.

- Self-sufficient school leaders have a fear of failure just like everyone else, *but* they fear *not* trying to succeed even more, so that is their prevalent instinct.
- Asking for support builds self-reliance.
- An aversion to asking for help causes isolation, separation and fragmentation.
- Ask for support when you know you don't have the capacity, knowledge or skillset required.
- Asking for help makes other people feel valued.
- Support is a two-way street. You must give in order to receive.
- You need a balance of support from different people in order to be resilient.
- Social media is a powerful tool for teachers to support one another, regardless of physical distance.

---

7 A sense of fun

It stands to reason that anyone who learns to live well will die well. The skills are the same: being present in the moment, and humble, and brave, and keeping a sense of humour.

Victoria Moran

And so, we arrive at one of the most difficult balloons to keep inflated in hard times, and yet one of the most important: a sense of fun. I am often asked whether, given my period of stress- and anxiety-related illness ten years ago, if I had my time again, I would have gone into teaching and into school leadership in particular?

My answer is always, 'Yes!' I had some great times in a career that spanned over a quarter of a century. I spent 23 years in senior leadership roles across four schools. I have just worked out that equates to 69 terms (which is a little unfortunate!). Of those 69, there were six that I found particularly challenging. Maths is not my strong suit, but I make that nine per cent. That's not bad odds, is it?

When you look back over a career of that length, inevitably you will remember the low points, but it is also the sound of laughter that you remember. The silly moments when things don't quite work out, or something quite unexpected happens.

In my first year of teaching, I clearly remember a boy called Shane bringing in a new pencil case that he had found under his Mum's bed but was struggling to open. Only it wasn't a pencil case (unless Ann Summers were diversifying their range!). I struggled to keep a straight face. I took it to the staffroom at lunch. I shared my tale gleefully but had to confess that I didn't know how to make 'the pencil case' work. I remember quite a prim teacher called Barbara grabbing it from my hand and saying, 'It's simple. You just twist the base like this!'

The 'pencil case' came to life. Barbara went pale and then slowly a vivid scarlet as the room went silent and every single member of staff turned towards her in amazement.

My leadership roles were serious. I wanted to make a positive difference in children's lives and I carried out my responsibilities diligently, but I certainly wasn't afraid of showing my lighter side, particularly on occasions such as 'Children in Need' and 'Comic Relief'. I have worn my clothes back to front, dressed as a woman, sung karaoke (my duet rendition of Elton John and Kiki Dee's *Don't go breaking my heart* was a triumph!) and I have been 'custard pied' more times than I care to remember, and always to the screaming delight of the kids (and probably the staff!). The most notable occasion was when somebody decided to use squirty cream rather than shaving foam. People were giving me a very wide berth by the end of the day because I smelt rancid.

You, dear reader, I am sure will have done many such similar things. These are the things that will stay with you and you will recall fondly as you look back on your career. School leadership is a challenging endeavour at times, but it is fun times like this that make it worthwhile. You need to have (and maintain) a sense of fun!

Time to reflect

Try to recall a humorous incident from an early point in your career.

- What happened and how did you feel?

- Why do you think this particular incident has stuck with you, when the lessons you taught that week, or the other activities you engaged in, probably haven't?

A sense of humour is part of the art of leadership, of getting along with people, of getting things done.

Dwight D. Eisenhower

A time and a place

A sense of humour in a school environment is very tricky to get right, particularly if you are in a leadership position. Leaders need to display dignity and some gravitas. A school leader who is forever cracking one-liners in meetings is unlikely to inspire confidence.

I once worked with a middle leader called Stuart. He was a nice enough guy and a good teacher but desperate to be popular and was armed with a veritable arsenal of one-liners to fit any occasion. In a one-to-one conversation it was tolerable, because you could deflect him and lead the conversation back to the original point. However, in meetings it was different. You would be discussing quite a serious point and his brain would make a link to a joke and out it would come. One or two people might smile or chuckle, but as time went by this habit began to grate on people and his interjections were increasingly met with an awkward silence, before someone would say, 'So anyway…'.

I know that our headteacher at the time popped round to Stuart's classroom after one such meeting. I assume that she 'had a word with him' because Stuart was very quiet in the next staff meeting and he reined in the humour in subsequent meetings. It was never that people disliked him, but because he made light of everything some people assumed that he did not take his job seriously. This was not true, yet it was a perception largely held by the people who did not work closely with him on a day-to-day basis; it was the image that he sometimes projected and it was not one that was particularly helpful to his own reputation and credibility with the wider staff of the school.

Levity has its place, but it is not generally in meetings.

Nor does it have much of a place in interview situations.

I spent over 20 years in senior leadership roles in large primary schools; combine that with many years helping to interview prospective initial teacher training candidates at the University of Derby, and I guess I have interviewed hundreds of people. In that time, I have seen many people try to crack a joke or be funny. When the attempted humour falls flat (which it generally does), the candidates often become flustered, as they know that they have misread the situation, and rarely regain their composure. Derby University very kindly pay me to deliver sessions on interview technique to their final year students and I always counsel against cracking jokes. It is such a difficult thing to pull off when you don't know your audience and how they are likely to respond.

The one occasion I can recall when it went down really well was in my first headship.

We were interviewing for a class teacher and there was a young Irish guy called Gordon, who had a winning smile and a bit of a twinkle in his eye. He also had the gift of the gab. He had sat cross-legged for much of the interview and the entire panel must have noticed that he had quite a big hole in the leather sole of his slightly battered brown brogues. He had interviewed well and at the end of the panel interview I asked him if he had anything else that he would like to add, which he had not had the opportunity to say.

'Please give me the job, I need some new shoes,' he replied.

We all laughed, Gordon included. It was a thoroughly charming moment. He had nailed it, but he had waited until he had weighed up the panel and the mood in the room before going for it.

Needless to say, he got the job.

Gordon went on to become a very successful primary headteacher.

I think part of the reason that humour can be a little bit tricky is because humour often has a bit of an edge to it. Think of stand-up comedians, for example. How many stand-up comedians can you think of whom you would be truly happy for your own young children to watch? Michael McIntyre, Tim Vine and Milton Jones would be contenders for me, but the vast majority walk a very fine line of taste and often get away with things that the rest of us might think but probably daren't say. Taste is a very individual thing. Even the wonderful Peter Kay, who has such a broad cross-generational appeal, walks that same line. I will never forget the scene from *Car Share* where they inadvertently drive off from the safari park with a stowaway monkey. The scene cuts from a shot of John and Kayleigh deep in discussion in the front of the car to a shot of the monkey 'enjoying himself' rather too much in the back. I was crying with laughter but it might not have been to everybody's taste.

I heard Matt Lucas being interviewed on the radio the other day. He was talking about the fact that it was ten years since he and David Walliams had done the *Little Britain* arena tour. He went on to say that even only a decade later, he did not believe that they would get away with poking fun at certain groups of people in society, as sensitivities and sensibilities have changed.

> *Humour, by its nature, tends to have an edge to it, so people typically tone it down at work. It's hard to do well and easy to do badly.*
>
> Laura Vanderkam (2013)

Given the quote above, it is easy to see why school leaders would not want to run the risk of causing offence to anyone and therefore avoid the use of humour. Add to this that schools are working environments that are mostly populated by children and thus you can't get away with using some kinds of language or humour. Add to this further with budget cuts, increasing levels of accountability and workload and it is easy to see how some schools have become rather joyless places to work in!

Sometimes as leaders, we can take ourselves way too seriously and want others to take us seriously as well.

Early on in my career I worked under a head of key stage, who we will call Cathy. Cathy was the most regimented person I have ever worked with. Her desk was always pristine, she was always on top of things and that's good. (You should see the state of my desk right now – it is covered in books, sheets of paper and coffee cups – as usual!) Cathy never came to staff socials or down to the pub on a Friday lunchtime (common practice back then) and she didn't even crack a smile at the pencil case incident that I mentioned above. She took herself way too seriously and, as a result, the younger members of staff in particular didn't take her very seriously. We used to have bets on who could make her crack a smile.

I don't think I ever managed it.

Sometimes people tone their sense of humour right down when they are in school because they desperately want colleagues and students to take them seriously. However, as Michael Kerr, International Business Speaker, says, 'This can backfire as people who take themselves overly seriously are often, ironically, taken less seriously by the people around them.' (Kerr, 2015)

Time to reflect

- Was there ever a time when you took yourself a little too seriously?
- What happened?
- What did you learn about yourself and other people as a result?
- Given your time again, what would you do differently?

So why is humour so important in schools?

Tasteful humour is an important factor in creating a happy environment in school where both pupils and staff can flourish and, as with most things, the tone is set by the leadership team.

Michael Kerr (2015) explains that in many organisations leaders cite a lack of time as one of the main dampening factors. People know that humour is good for morale and the desire is there, but they just don't know how to bring more humour and joy into their busy working lives. To stay resilient yourself, as well as build the resilience of the staff you lead, you need to find the time to explore the lighter side of teaching.

As a leader, being able to find humour even when the going is tough is really important. It allows you to step outside yourself for a moment and find some perspective when otherwise you 'cannot see the wood for the trees'.

I am not suggesting that you should start every meeting with a joke, but a little self-deprecating humour or gently poking fun at an outside influence that people find stressful can genuinely help people feel better about their situation. For example, when Michael Gove was Minister of State for Education in England, Amazon did a roaring trade in a book supposedly written by Mr Gove himself entitled *Everything I Know About Teaching*; the book was completely blank inside.

A sense of fun, led from the top, can make a huge difference to the culture of any organisation, not least schools.

When the hugely successful American company Southwest Airlines was formed in the early 1970s, air travel was largely the province of the white upper and middle classes. Southwest started with a clear sense of purpose: to make air travel affordable to all and to make it fun!

Southwest have a very brave management system. Provided that they fulfil their statutory responsibilities, they trust and encourage their flight crew to use their individual talents to communicate with and engage with their passengers.

If you can bear to tear yourself away from this chapter for a few minutes, check out the following links on YouTube and you will see what I mean.

- 'Flight attendant RAPPING the safety briefing! South West Airlines!'
  www.youtube.com/watch?v=DYA_ivyj3kE&t=25s
- 'Hilarious Southwest flight attendant'
  www.youtube.com/watch?v=07LFBydGjaM&t=90s
- 'Funniest Southwest Airlines flight attendants Frank and Clarence'
  www.youtube.com/watch?v=_F_n09WMV6Y&t=1s

- 'One of Southwest Airlines' singing flight attendants!' www.youtube.com/watch?v=Jy0Yf1CAsuQ

Okay, they are rather American in style and I am not advocating that you rap your way through next week (they will cart you off in a van if you do). My point is this: the last time I flew, I was greeted politely as I got on the plane and I settled myself down in my seat and looked over the safety instructions tucked into the pocket of the seat in front. (I am a nervous flyer and a bit like a member of 'The A-Team'; you have to ply me with a whisky before I board, and I need to know where the emergency exits are!)

As the cabin crew gave the safety talk, I paid great attention, even though I had seen such demonstrations many times before. However, towards the end I glanced around the plane and realised that the vast majority of people were paying little or no attention to what was being said. Most were either in conversation, buried in a book or texting.

Now, if you have had a chance to check out the video links above, you will, I am sure, have noticed that the vast majority of passengers on the Southwest planes are paying attention and are fully engaged. The airline has huge customer loyalty and they have clearly learned the importance of a sense of fun when delivering information.

Since Southwest was formed, many people have tried to replicate the formula, but they have concentrated on the cost-cutting element of it rather than the sense of fun, with varying degrees of success.

Some of you may remember Laker Airways. Founded by Sir Freddy Laker in the late 1970s, Laker Airways was one of the first 'no-frills' airlines operating between Gatwick and New York. It caught the public imagination briefly but struggled in the UK recession of the early 1980s when people were feeling the pinch and were less inclined to travel. It spectacularly and very publicly went bankrupt in 1982. Now, bearing in mind that I can rarely remember what happened last week let alone over 35 years ago, it is indicative of the level of coverage that this event received that I can still remember the six o'clock BBC News bulletin announcing their demise (other news providers are available although less so back then – we didn't even have Channel 4 until the autumn of that year!).

Ryanair have similarly based themselves on a 'no-frills approach', and despite negative press about baggage 'add-ons' and cancelled flights, they manage to maintain customer loyalty due to very competitive prices, but as to a sense of fun…?

On a practical level, humour is a potent reliever of stress. Work-related stress is one of the biggest causes of staff absence in school. This can have a huge financial impact on schools, but it can also have an effect on other colleagues, who may have to explain to supply or cover staff what needs to be done each day, adding to their own workload. Most importantly, it can have a significant impact on the children, their education and the school's results.

Surely creating a sense of fun in schools, where we work hard but play hard, can only contribute to reducing absence, as there are many physical and mental benefits associated with laughter.

When I was growing up, my grandma would always tell me that 'laughter is the best medicine'. I am sure that I must have rolled my eyes on more than one occasion, but she was a wise lady and what she told me is true.

Laughter relieves stress, elevates mood and makes you more resilient.

The benefits of laughter

- **Firstly, laughter helps to relax the muscles throughout the body** – A good belly laugh helps to relieve muscular tension and stress, leaving your muscles relaxed for up to 45 minutes.
- **The act of laughing triggers the release of endorphins, our natural feel-good chemicals** – Endorphins help to create an overall sense of wellbeing and can even help with short-term pain relief.
- **Laughter can help to boost your immune system** – It does this by decreasing stress hormones and increasing your immune cells and infection-fighting antibodies. This, in turn, improves your resistance to infections and diseases.
- **Laughter improves the function of blood vessels in the heart** – The increased blood flow can help protect you against the risks of a heart attack and other cardiovascular problems.
- **Laughter burns calories** – Now I'm not suggesting that if you laugh a lot you are necessarily going to drop a dress or collar size, nor am I suggesting that it would replace going to the gym or other vigorous exercise, but to borrow Tesco's slogan for a moment: 'Every little helps!'
- **Laughter is a powerful tool for managing conflict** – Carefully placed humour can help to reduce tension between members of your team

when emotions are running high. A shared laugh, in some situations, can diffuse anger and conflict quickly, bring everyone's stress levels down a notch or two and help get back to communicating in a way that is more helpful. It can help people to move on from a confrontation without being bitter or resentful.

- **Laughter is contagious** – This is one good reason why most TV sitcoms use laughter tracks or, in some cases (*Mrs Brown's Boys*, for example), record in front of a live studio audience. You are far more likely to laugh if you hear other people laughing 'around you' than if you are sat in a room on your own. Your own ability to laugh at a situation, or indeed yourself, has a positive ripple effect on other people.

Ultimately, people want to work with people they like. It's not rocket science. You spend a lot of time in school and the days go by so much more quickly if there is a little levity. People don't want to see work as a 'death march' down the long road to retirement. It is a skill, but leaders who are able to deftly employ some humour in their work stand a good chance of creating genuine respect (as opposed to a climate of fear) and are more likely to successfully influence the views of others. The rules, though, as Laura Vanderkam wisely says, are as follows: 'You need to be funny, but not snarky (that's not good for team building) and you can't offend anyone.' (Vanderkam, 2013)

Paul Osincup in his TEDx speech 'Leading with laughter: The power of humor in leadership' suggests that people are crying out for leaders who are relatable, imperfect and, on occasion, a little bit silly. How seriously other people take us is of inverse proportion to how seriously we take ourselves, he suggests.

A good sense of humour has become a must-have for leaders to effectively deal with employees, subordinates and workplace crisis.

Neha Singh Verma (2013)

Many years ago, I visited a large inner city junior school. I cannot actually remember the purpose of my visit in all honesty, but there are two things that I do remember about the visit. The first was driving up and parking in a side street and staring up at the monolithic, two-storey, Victorian red-brick facade. It was very imposing! The second thing that I remember was being taken on a tour of the building by a member of staff. We had just climbed the stone steps to the first-floor landing. Ahead was a solid wood door marked 'Headteacher's Office'. It had a strange look of foreboding. I was talking to my guide but at the same time, over his shoulder, I saw a hapless young teacher with a pile of folders under one arm timidly approach the door. She knocked gently.

'GO AWAY!!!!' boomed a low female voice from within! The headteacher clearly!

The young teacher scurried away like a startled dormouse.

'Take no notice!' muttered my guide. 'She's always doing it.'

The head could not have had any idea whether it was a pupil or a member of staff that had dared to approach her lair, although in truth, nobody deserves to be spoken to or be treated in that way. When I saw her steam her way down the corridors of the school and into the school hall to take assembly, I noted that she was every bit as imposing and intimidating as the building itself.

I would not have liked to have knocked on her door. Nor would I like to have uttered the words, 'Could you help me? I need some advice?' Or worse still, 'I have a bit of a problem...'

Thankfully, the culture in schools has mostly changed in the intervening years.

School leaders need to be approachable. A good sense of humour therefore plays a big role in ensuring that a leader is perceived as someone with whom members of staff can share their concerns and discuss their problems. Humour encourages connectivity between staff members and promotes a sense that 'we are all in this together'. It also allows a free flow of ideas, suggestions and creative inputs within your team. It moves a school away from a situation where its leaders feel under tremendous pressure to 'have all the answers' and encourages collective ownership of the challenges that need to be faced.

Not everything in school goes to plan (you may have noticed this phenomenon!). In some ways, it is like working in a hospital. You start off a shift with a plan but pretty soon something will transpire that serves to blow your balloon off course. When school leaders can recognise this fact, and see the lighter or humorous aspects of unplanned-for outcomes and situations, they are far better equipped to attract (and retain) like-minded, resilient individuals as well as build loyal teams. For the same reason, schools that have leaders that possess and demonstrate a sense of humour are better equipped to weather a storm of the unexpected, rather than be broken by it.

It's not just about cracking jokes

You really don't need to be cracking jokes every five minutes to create a happy environment in your school. It's the little things, like socials, for example. We used to go tenpin bowling followed by a visit to Pizza Express. In my first headship we went paintballing together as a staff. In a reckles attempt to 'demonstrate my leadership style', I charged the 'enemy' camp drawing fire, whilst others from my team went around the sides and captured the enemy flag. We succeeded and very nobly I sacrificed myself for the greater good. Even with a mask, I had so many bruises around the throat the next day that some of the parents thought that I had actually been assaulted. We also had 'secret angels' every now and then, where you secretly drew the name of a member of staff, and had to do something 'nice' for them every day for a week, until they had to 'guess who' on the Friday. A sense of fun is about creating a pleasant working environment and a sense of community. This can make the difference between getting through tough times together, or not.

As an interim head, Patrick Ottley-O'Connor is often working in situations where schools need to make rapid improvements. Inevitably there is pressure, but he does not lose sight of the need to have fun. When I last met him, he was not in a position to pay staff for Year 11 revision sessions, so he entered all the staff who volunteered to deliver the sessions into a prize draw, 'The wheel of misfortune'. Potential prizes included strawberries and cream served by members of the senior leadership team (it was Wimbledon fortnight), a candlelit dinner for two with the Principal(!) or a pair of plimsolls (or pumps depending on which part of the UK you live in). I have a phobia of pumps! As a student, I once had a summer job working in a warehouse peeling sticky price labels off the things. They had been imported from Taiwan with the wrong price on and it was my job to stick the right one on. (That is ten weeks of my life I will never get back!)

Patrick places a star under one seat at staff meetings. Whoever finds the star wins a random prize. At Friday briefings, a spin of a wheel decides which member of staff receives a box of chocolates. There is also a wellbeing star of the week where staff can nominate someone who has made a positive impact on the mental health and wellbeing of others. This could be won for all manner of reasons, e.g.

- A member of staff whose mum had died and who had been off work for ten days found that when she came back, her faculty had marked all her books for her.

- One heavily pregnant teacher nominated two colleagues because she was struggling getting a box of books out of her car one morning. One helped her by carrying in the books whilst another made and brought her a cup of tea.

Patrick's current school have a wellbeing Advent calendar. Opening a door might reveal a suggestion such as 'Compliment someone' or 'Sit at lunch with someone you have not sat with before' or 'Make a phone call home to praise a student.'

Patrick agrees that there was some cynicism at this approach at the beginning but notes that as time goes by, people have really started to value it. He adds that, 'What we have done to play and enjoy will take us through any dark period.'

Summary

- **Laughter has multiple health benefits, including muscle relaxation, reducing the impacts of stress and an improved immune system and cardiovascular function.**
- **A sense of humour is integral to effective school leadership, relating to other people and getting things done.**
- **Leaders who are able to deftly employ some humour in their work stand a good chance of creating genuine respect and are more likely to successfully influence the views of others.**
- **Humour needs to be kept within the bounds of dignity and should not be offensive or involve putting other people down. It also has a time and a place.**
- **Self-deprecating humour allows us to step outside of our immediate situation and affords some objectivity. It also humanises leaders.**
- **Humour helps staff to feel that school leaders are approachable and builds trust. This in turn allows for an open exchange of ideas, building collaboration.**
- **Laughter is a powerful tool for managing conflict.**
- **Schools that have leaders that possess and demonstrate a sense of humour are better equipped to weather a storm of the unexpected.**
- **How seriously other people take us is in inverse proportion to how seriously we take ourselves.**
- **Tasteful humour is an important factor in creating a happy environment in school where both pupils and staff can flourish.**
- **As with most things, the tone is set by the leadership team.**

8 Curiosity

Curiosity is the engine of achievement.

Sir Ken Robinson

Our eighth balloon of resilience is curiosity. Take yourself to one of those dark days: midwinter, post-Christmas. The rain is running down your office window, the sky is leaden and dark, and it's only 11am. You've dealt with an irate parent and a frazzled teaching assistant who is going to have to cover the class of one of the teachers who seems to have persistent flu, and it's data day… again! You've got three policies that urgently need reviewing, a head's report to write for the governors and an anticipated Ofsted inspection that is merely a phone call away.

It wasn't how the day had been planned during your semi-conscious battle to get to sleep the previous evening, with your *Fitbit* obsession sending you desperately on the quest for more than one hour of 'deep sleep'. Today was supposed to be a day of gentle reflection, some 'you time', a cup of proper coffee, maybe even some Ludovico Einaudi playing in the background of your office and a couple of hours to feel proactive.

The fact that the day hasn't mapped out like that doesn't surprise you though; you've been planning one for months – no, years – but it's always been tantalisingly out of reach.

Have you ever wondered why, in American politics, they talk so much about the 'first hundred days' of a president's tenure? Why here, and probably in most democracies to be fair, governments seem destined to lose power, despite the hope and optimism that often follows an election victory (at least from their own supporters)?

Why the first hundred days? Because it's said that the job is so big, so complex and so full on that it's the only time the new incumbent will have to actively pursue their own agenda, their 'visionary' programme. From the hundred and first day, they will be swamped by their in tray full of all the domestic and international issues they have to respond to. Whatever happened to Mr Trump's wall? The same is true in the UK. Governments drive hard at their manifesto pledges – the headline-making elements of their election campaigns – to begin with, but after a short time their agendas get overtaken by other issues – BREXIT, for example. For the rest of us, going about our everyday lives, it just feels very much like the same old thing.

For companies like Google and Apple the challenge has been their success, their stratospheric rise with nothing to lose on the way up, but once they're there, the pressure becomes about maintenance – staying there, responding to the needs of customers and shareholders and staying ahead of the competition.

If not in politics, how about in sport? A football manager arrives at a new club with flashbulbs, Twitter likes and supporters' chants ringing in their ears. They often win their first few games – a new era has dawned – but within a matter of months, it's all gone south. Think of Claudio Ranieri's tenure at Leicester City, for example. Talk about 'hero to zero'!

You see it in business too. Eric Schmidt, until very recently the Executive Chairman of Google, has said on many occasions that his greatest challenges over his years with the company have been to keep the dynamic, forward-thinking momentum going. Steve Jobs too was always terrified of Apple becoming a company that simply made stuff, rather than inventing it.

Time to reflect

When was the last time you blocked an hour out of your day at work just to think, to research, to stare out of a window, to allow yourself to dwell a little on the past and how you felt on your first day in your current post at your current school?

- **Find yourself some evocative music and do it now.**

Visualise the day you were actually appointed, remember the feelings and emotions and also the dreams you had for what you wanted to achieve.

- Jot them down

- Do a quick audit. How are you doing?

From proactive to reactive

Looking back on my first role in senior leadership, and actually in headship, I felt a conflicting mixture of arrogance and ignorance. I was so ready for it; I'd seen others in the role and knew the behaviours I would try to emulate as well as those that I would certainly avoid! I felt that I was ready, but despite my experiences to date, you can never really know what lies ahead and the impact that that ultimate position of responsibility carries. Even two stints as an acting head did not fully prepare me for headship.

In the early days of any new job we are fully energised, excited and probably a little idealistic. It's the same for many at the start of a new year. We've sung *Auld Lang Syne*, watched the fireworks and counted down the bongs of Big Ben and drunk some fizz. We are ready. This year is going to be the year – it's all ahead of us: more fun, more exercise, less cake, more veg and definitely less stress!

Our new job, like the new year, comes with a feeling of a clean slate; the exhaustion and reactive actions of the old are gone; fresh energy, fresh start; it's time to be in control again.

Eventually, we all become **REACTIVE**.

This is not to criticise or even to pretend it's avoidable, but it is so important that we are able to recognise it explicitly, to monitor it and to become disciplined enough to do something about it.

As we have already recognised in this book, school leadership is tough; it's all-consuming and driven by a passion to do the best for your community, your colleagues and your students. We are a profession largely cursed with two things: firstly, impostor syndrome – someday soon, someone is going to find out that I have weaknesses and other people may be better at some aspects of my job than I am – and secondly, guilt – whatever you've done, it's never enough; it could have and should have been better.

Teachers are extraordinary people; it's why what you do can never be seen as just a job with fixed hours or job descriptions. Good teachers are extraordinarily self-sacrificing; others always come first, sometimes to the detriment of yourself and your own family.

So we never stop driving ourselves to feel of value, worthy of the trust of those who rely on us. We are obsessed with making good for all around us and it can, and often does, lead us into a tunnel.

Do you remember your first day as a fully-fledged teacher? The resources you bought or made, the displays that were triple mounted, laminated and perfectly centred? The child you had been briefed about who was a 'nightmare' but whom you were going to transform? The joy those early days brought you? What happened?

What many of us forget about our teacher training is how proactive it was. Even in the heart of our school practices we had time, time to talk to our peers, to sit cross-legged in our student digs making stuff, planning stuff and exploring the future.

To an extent, the same was true as you prepared for leadership: time spent talking about the future, about how you would do it differently, what your school might look like.

When you think about it, our professional progress and development is much like the growth of a child. Our early years, if we are lucky, are spent in stimulating environments, filled with awe and wonder; everything is new, everything is questioned. Our lives are filled with new sights, sounds and experiences. We soak it all up like a sponge. It's actually miraculous when you think about the development of a young child; most of us learn to walk and talk, to form relationships and manipulate our environments. Then it all slows down a little; we find learning harder and harder. Language acquisition, for example: sure, as young children, our neurons are firing and our brain is yet to rationalise where to expend its energy, but we pick up every language spoken in our home. At nursery and then school, most of us learn to pick up reading and writing quickly and then it all seems to slow down a little; it all seems to become that much harder. It is one of the reasons I gave up amateur dramatics as I got older. At the age of 20 I could memorise two pages of dialogue from a script in two or three rehearsals. By the age of 40 it was taking me two or three weeks! As we get older, we start to talk increasingly about time being a major factor in why we don't learn or experience new things as often or as easily as we would like.

As young children we are incredibly proactive; as new teachers we are the same and, for most of us, early leadership roles are filled with the newness that stimulates.

We have the time, energy and confidence to be CURIOUS

With that curiosity comes a certain amount of resilience. As a young child, for example, if we turn down a dead end, we may cry a little (okay, I cried a lot), but very soon we are off on another journey, driven by a new question, by the desire to learn and be more. As young teachers we are confident enough to ask, to question, to admit our weaknesses in a desire to improve and to learn. As young leaders we happily ask advice of more experienced colleagues. It's okay to not know and to show curiosity. I was fortunate to have other, experienced heads who were more than happy to be at the end of a telephone and help me with procedures I did not understand or offer advice on situations I had not encountered before.

Whilst you never stop learning as a school leader, there comes a point when you have been doing the job a while, when you do start to feel that you should (and other people expect you to) have all the answers.

Time to reflect

- Be honest with yourself; when was the last time you responded to not knowing something with a feeling of enthusiasm?

- What were the circumstances?

- **What was it about the situation that caught your imagination?**

So many of us start heading down a tunnel; it often starts with a feeling of 'busy': when I clear my desk, my diary, once this issue is dealt with, when Ofsted have been (and gone!), then I will get around to…

We see the pressure on our colleagues and want to do something to alleviate their stress or concern.

The first thing to get jettisoned is the meeting you didn't really want to go to anyway, so that's okay. Then maybe the coffee you have once a term with the peer you got to know earlier in your career, the one person you can be professionally honest and open with. Then you set the alarm earlier in the morning to get in further ahead of the day; you cancel gym memberships or evening recreation (amateur dramatics in my case) because you need to work the extra hours, in order to keep your head above water.

It doesn't take long until all the proactivity has gone; every minute of every day now feels like survival: the day, the week, the term, the year. It can become about 'destination addiction', just getting through to the next holiday. Many teachers can tell you exactly how many weeks and days it is until the next break. The tragedy of it all is that when you do get there, you are too emotionally drained to take any time for yourself. Now you are almost completely reactive.

The supreme irony is that being reactive is so much more exhausting than being proactive. For years in schools and colleges, we have talked about being burnt out by change. We are desperate for it to end. Interestingly, it isn't all change that exhausts us; it is the reactive changes that dominate our jobs. Government policy, it seems to me, is very rarely proactive; our own school development plans tend to be dominated by responding to events, environments or data. Change very rarely feels exciting or dynamic; for most of us it actually constitutes more work, more complexity, more exhaustion; in truth, it's why so many of us become cynical or even resentful of 'the system'. The magic of our youthful arrogance and ignorance has long since faded or become jaded.

One of the core problems with curiosity is that it is seen by many, as we get older, as a luxury item – something that is only there for the time-rich or the young. To an extent, it's the way we were taught as children ourselves.

Those of you who have had children of your own go through the education system will know what I mean. As our kids get older and the educational stakes get higher, we see them spend more and more time studying in their rooms or at the dining table and, sadly, less and less time doing the things that they love.

Are we trained out of being curious?

As a school leader, would you ever take time, during the school day, to read a book or an article? Would you take time to leave the premises for a coffee and a chat with a colleague from another school? If not, why not?

Is it guilt?

'I have to be here; I'm indispensable; I can't be seen to be doing something that isn't directly measurable or commensurate with stress and pressure on my staff.'

Is it fear?

'I might be seen by a parent or governor; they would jump to the wrong conclusions.'

Is it time?

'I have got so much on my "to do list" to get done, time out will just put more pressure on me and lead to greater stress.'

All of these are perfectly valid, especially if you regard the process of stimulating your curiosity as a luxury and, maybe provocatively, have the belief that your job isn't actually about leadership but management. There is no doubt that managing our schools is both time-consuming and vital; it takes the vast majority of our time and energy, but leadership is vital and needs nurturing. In some ways, it is the difference between reactive and proactive actions.

> *Management works in the system; leadership works on the system.*
>
> Stephen Covey (2004b)

Most of us chose school leadership to be involved in exactly that, because you feel productive and useful and, to be honest, it makes your heart beat a little faster. It is exhausting but in a positive way.

One of the traits of a great teacher is someone who, first and foremost, has a love of learning, and learning is of course driven by curiosity; the resulting discovery is not only life-affirming but addictive and energising.

To ensure that there is light in your tunnel, you need the spark of curiosity that will ignite your environment and, vicariously, the environment of others (colleagues, community and students).

The danger in our world is that we focus relentlessly in the system, not on it. This brings me to the most important distinction between reactive and proactive process and the comparative mental and physical impact. To be reactive is, for the most part, to feel out of control, which in itself is a major catalyst for stress, whereas being proactive largely implies that you are in control of actions. For most of us in education, change feels reactive, regularly underlining our perceived lack of control, which in turn cultivates stress, scepticism and downright anger. Being proactive makes us feel empowered, valued and professional.

In order to cultivate a feeling of proactivity, we need to find the time and space to ask questions, to stimulate our thinking and to develop our actions – this, of course, with having the time and giving ourselves the permission to be curious.

I asked Ross Morrison McGill what he thought about the importance of curiosity as a trait in school leaders. This is his response.

I believe it is hugely important; right up there with desirable leadership qualities. Without getting too much into the research of growth mindset versus fixed mindset, some people are just lacking the passion to ask questions, to learn and act in a curious manner; they are quite happy with what they have got. I think of myself as a curious person. I love connecting with other people, reading other people's blogs, collaborating on books and articles because I am hungry to learn. We only have one life, none of us have all the answers, but we should leave planet Earth having contributed in our own way.

We are living in more complicated times; a smaller and rapidly connected world. Yet, why do we feel we work within a more fragmented education system? At the time of writing, Multi-Academy Trusts for example, are changing the educational landscape, but also in this new digital epoch, with social media, we can connect and be curious with one another. People can now collaborate online very quickly and ask valid questions about evidence and say, its impact. All good questions to ask.

I was recently at an event where Mark Stevenson, a London-based British author, businessman, public speaker and futurologist – yes, that's his job title – was talking about system change and 'participation virus'. There are many curious people in the social media community, who want to be the first one to post an interesting image or video. We want to make it easy for other people to become involved. This curiosity leads us to explore for example, what happens in a good school? What happens in a great school? Why does this school leader work in this way?

Whilst some people just want to turn up to do the job and go home, others are up for the challenge and will do whatever they can to make things better for students despite the odds being stacked against them and their cohort. Early adopters of new ideas and approaches want to ask more reliable questions about the current model of our education system. The context in which we work affects our curiosity. If I am a leader in an outstanding school or one in special measures, what I am curious about may be very different. Either way, we must use this curiosity to develop the profession as a whole, rather than seek to attain any accolades for a system that currently only recognises schools who fall on the better half of the bell curve.

Ross Morrison McGill

Sometimes our situation inevitably forces us into reactive behaviours. Most such behaviours tend to be closed in terms of answers, outcomes or actions. Proactivity is more open-ended; to be curious is to ask open-ended questions where there is no predefined, fixed answer; it often leads to more questions and further developments.

I remember, as a young teacher preparing for my first round of interviews for my first leadership post, being coached to respond to questions in a proactive way. If, for example, I was asked how I would deal with a child who had run away, I needed to demonstrate three responses: the first two should be largely reactive and short- and medium-term actions; the third, which was really the sign of leadership, should be long-term and more proactive:

- So, the first action would be to phone the parents or carers to see if the child had returned home, to send a member of staff out to trace the potential routes the child might take and, if necessary, to call the police.
- The second action would be to discuss with the staff and parents what had happened, why and what must be done to prevent the incident recurring.
- The third action would be to develop strategies, working with the students and staff, to pre-empt the need to flee and to explore alternatives to running off – for example a cool-off space, a counsellor or a buddy system.

These are not necessarily the only answers but interestingly, later in my career when I was interviewing potential leadership candidates, they would go through the process of actions one and two but rarely three. Now, on reflection, there is an extension to action three or even an action four: looking at how others do it. Not just in schools, but in care homes, young offenders' institutions, etc.?

Curiosity isn't mystical or complicated, but it does require work and stimulation and, dare I say it, it needs you to get in touch with the childlike curiosity of your younger days. If you are fortunate to work in a school with an Early Years unit, paying regular visits there to spend time with the children is often a great start point.

Learning from others

You know that clichéd saying, 'I wish I knew then what I know now'? Well, I feel like that all the time. Since leaving headship, I have spent an increasing amount of time with people who work in a variety of settings, not just educational, and working, observing and talking with them has stimulated my thinking in a way that I wish I had valued as a school leader. My friend and former colleague, Richard Gerver, would often visit organisations outside of education to generate ideas for development in his school. I remember on one occasion, during work to develop a more productive culture, he visited a local call centre where the company had found a way to create a stimulating and dynamic working environment for the (often) young people working in what was otherwise, for many, a monotonous job with many rejections. On another occasion he visited the Microsoft campus near Reading to find ideas for developing an environment focused on the achievement of excellence whilst maintaining a culture of fun, innovation and creativity. The stimulation gained in such visits helped to shape many of the innovations at his school, Grange Primary.

Many of us will feel comfortable visiting or sending our staff to visit other schools in the hope that we can bring back ideas based on best practice, but we should avoid falling into the trap of believing that we can only make our schools or ourselves better by spending our professional time with people who do what we do. Indeed, some of the time management tips I found most useful as a head I gained from an exchange programme with a manager of a local industry and from someone I met who was a chief superintendent in the police!

Google and Pixar invest millions of dollars in providing their employees with learning experiences that often have nothing to do with their jobs, constantly encouraging them to try new things and to meet new people from outside of their working environment, not because they want to be 'nice' but because it has a massive impact on productivity and sustainable development.

Before you start shouting at me, I am not saying that we, in our schools, can do anything like that, but the principles are strong and we can develop strategies that stimulate and feed our own curiosity, help re-energise and therefore feed our resilience.

In essence, in order to develop a culture that encourages curiosity we need to do nothing more than celebrate learning, encouraging questions, risk and exploration – processes we implement every day in our classrooms, with our students.

The key starting point is time; isn't it always?

Your first job, as has come up so many times in this book, is to model the behaviour, which means that you need to be seen to be taking time to question and explore, sharing your experiences with colleagues. Have you thought, for example, of asking a governor with an interesting job if you could visit their place of work for a tour and a chat? In my second headship we had a governor who worked for Toyota. I visited the plant in south Derbyshire. It was fascinating to see how their work processes are redesigned to eliminate 'muda' (waste) through the process of continuous review and improvement known as 'kaizen'. It did get me thinking about how we might reduce waste and save money back at school, and when the school won a National Lottery 'People's millions' bid to build a community wildlife and sensory garden, Toyota kindly released some of their workers to construct some raised planting beds as part of their community outreach programme.

Do you have friends or relatives who work in interesting environments? If so, it's the same idea.

The first thing I suspect you will notice is that the problems you are dealing with are not unique to you, to your school or even to education. That realisation is, in itself, both comforting and energising. Suddenly our tunnel is one that is shared; it's a little wider and not so dark or lonely.

Asking 'daft' questions

One of the greatest injections of energy into our schools comes when we get the chance to employ new staff – some fresh blood. As head of a very large school I was often in the fortunate position of being able to do this. It's often a confident and relentlessly curious NQT who makes a comment or an observation, early in their tenure, who stimulates new thinking. We are so busy doing what needs to be done, in the way it's always worked, that we find it hard to step back and view our processes with fresh and objective eyes, so it's worth getting trusted friends and governors to come into school and spend a few hours with you, observing. That way, they can ask the 'daft' questions that often turn out not to be daft at all and help to stimulate your own curiosity. However, you need to be open enough to hear stuff that may take you out of your comfort zone, and that is a massive challenge. Curiosity is not always comfortable, and you and your staff must be confident enough to take observations and ideas as a chance for some action research, as starting points to explore the merits, or otherwise, of new ways of thinking or new practices.

Curiosity must not lead to constantly existing in your comfort zone. One of the most successful traits of sustainably evolving organisations is the culture of challenge they promote. There is a real temptation in high-pressure environments to surround yourself with 'like-minded' people who all agree with each other all of the time. This will lead to a curiosity paralysis. It's like watching those couples who have been together a very long time enjoy a candlelit dinner on Valentine's evening at the next table to you, who sit and say nothing to each other, with the exception of commenting on the quality of the food.

> *Surrounding yourself with 'yes people' is like talking to yourself.*
>
> Frank Sonnenberg (2016)

It takes courage to step out of our comfort zone, but in a way, that is exactly what this book is about. Resilience is, to an extent, nurtured through self-action and the growing confidence to deal with the unexpected. Curiosity is the catalyst that allows us to move forward, to learn, to explore and to develop. It isn't a luxury but a necessity if we are to lead sustainable and resilient organisations.

What next?

1. On a personal level, if there's a local organisation you've always been fascinated by, bite the bullet, give them a ring, explain who you are and get over there. I think you may be surprised at how eager they are to help.
2. Plan for one staff meeting to be given over to exploring a daft question. Something like, how do we make our maths lessons more 'rock 'n' roll'?
3. Mix it up; run regular staff meetings where teachers interview teachers in other departments or age groups about what they do and how they do it. Set up a programme of peer class exchanges.
4. Start up a learning library where colleagues share books that stimulate their thinking; one caveat – they can't be books about teaching! (And no trashy fiction either!)

We are all familiar with the warning transmitted by the famous proverb, 'Curiosity killed the cat.' What is maybe more pertinent here is to delve into the proverb's origin. It first appeared in the play by Ben Jonson, written in 1598, called *Every Man in His Humour*, where the line actually stated, 'Care will kill a cat.' Care, as referred to, meant worry or sorrow, not curiosity. I would suggest that we avoid the same mistake. The way to avoid worry and sorrow is not to retreat into ourselves but instead to embrace curiosity and reach out to others.

In order to protect ourselves in times of sorrow or worry, we must not forgo or stifle our curiosity. It is vital that we energise ourselves through constant learning and development; it is important that we can step away from our problems and contextualise them. We feed our resilience by ensuring that we can remain proactive, by finding control and professional satisfaction through leadership and not just management. In the end it comes down to what defines us as educators and actually as human beings: our curiosity.

Summary

- Many school leaders start their role being proactive but over time shift to a more reactive style of leadership.
- Most reactive behaviours tend to be closed in terms of answers, outcomes or action.
- Proactivity is more open-ended; to be curious is to ask open-ended questions where there is no predefined, fixed answer.
- In order to cultivate a feeling of proactivity, we need to find the time and space to ask questions.
- With curiosity comes a certain amount of resilience.
- Learn from others through visits – a relatively cheap form of CPD – but don't restrict yourself to schools.
- Ask the 'daft' questions and avoid surrounding yourself with 'yes' people. It stifles creativity.
- We feed our resilience by ensuring that we can remain proactive, by finding control and professional satisfaction through leadership and not just management.

9 Taking care of yourself and others

Self-care is never a selfish act – it is simply good stewardship of the only gift I have, the gift I was put on earth to offer others.

Parker Palmer (1999)

We are nearing the end of our trip together, and we arrive at a balloon of paramount importance: taking care of yourself and others. School leaders need plans for everything these days, from school improvement plans, to what to do in what order should they receive that inspection call (see Chapter 10, p. 161), from fire evacuation plans to, more recently, lockdown procedures in the event of terrorists or intruders. However, how many of you out there have a plan for your own wellbeing? Not many, I suspect. Now take a look at your 'to do list'. How many of you have actually got anything written on it that it is to do with taking care of yourself?

Again, I suspect that the answer is painfully few! I'm not being critical here. For many years I was actually the same. Looking after myself was never very high up my list of priorities. I was, for ten years, running an exceptionally large primary school and my priority was looking after my pupils and staff. That amounted to around 900 people. That's a lot of people to try to take care of. I had many failings as a leader, I am sure, but I hope that my kids and staff would say that I cared. As Andy Cope suggests in his foreword (p. ix), perhaps I cared too much at times, but as he also says, it is better to be that way than not to give a damn! Still, it took up a lot of physical and emotional energy. I took up my first senior leadership role at 27, which in those days was certainly considered young, but successive headteachers saw potential in me that was matched with boundless enthusiasm and energy. Give me a project and I would run with it and see it through to the finish. I was seconded by the local authority on several occasions to support schools in difficulty and to support newly qualified teachers. I was pretty fearless back then (except about flying in planes, which fortunately is not generally a requirement in teaching!).

I drank lots of coffee, stayed up late, sometimes skipped meals and ate the wrong things (yes, even back then, it was always 'a bloody burger!') and drank a lot of beer at the weekends.

It was not a problem. But it is not sustainable – not in the long term.

By my mid-forties, my lack of self-care mixed in with increasing pressures at work made for a toxic combination. I struggled on in a state of wilful blindness, ignoring the building symptoms of migraines, back pain, panic attacks and a stammer. (This is all charted in much greater detail in my first book, *Leading From the Edge*. Don't be put off – it is an uplifting read with a happy ending!) The notion of taking care of myself and investing in my own wellbeing, perversely, seemed rather… well, selfish!

What a fool I had been, because when my symptoms came to a dramatic head (no pun intended here) I was off work and away from school for the best part of six months. My deputy and assistant head did a magnificent job of running the school in my absence and I will be forever grateful for that, but it significantly added to their responsibilities and pressure.

The moral of this story? Investing in your own wellbeing as a leader may seem selfish, but actually not doing so can prove rather more selfish in the long run.

Now, given that I certainly wasn't looking after myself ten years ago and given that I don't look exactly svelte even now, I don't want to set myself up as being some kind of wellbeing guru because that would be disingenuous. It is like putting the bins out. I know it's important, but I still forget to do it sometimes!

So, instead, I have turned here to a couple of people I know who *are* experts in the field.

Sharon de Caestecker and Elain Crewe run a Leicestershire-based company called WELLBEING4LIFE. They work alongside individuals and organisations including, more recently, with schools in terms of wellbeing. They take a very holistic approach as you will see if you take a look at their website: www.wellbeing-4-life.com.

I recently met up with Elain and Sharon to ask them their views. Now… ahem, I have a small confession here. I am somewhat forgetful at times and I forgot to bring anything to verbally record our discussion on, so ended up with written notes instead. I can't clearly remember which one of them said which bits, so for the purposes of the following, they conveniently speak as one! I ask forgiveness from Sharon and Elain themselves, from Hannah – my editor – and from you, the reader, for me being a bit rubbish. I promise that if I ever write a third book, I will do better!

Me:
To what extent do you think there is a link between a healthy body and a healthy mind?

Elain and Sharon:
Before we even get into the science, let's consider what it means to have a healthy body.

Imagine this. Our body is healthy and strong. We experience no pain and we have energy most of the time. We are able to choose to walk, exercise or generally just move in order to achieve what we need to in our lives, whether that is simply walking the dog, playing with the kids, walking around the shops or enjoying a run or an exercise class. There are no barriers to what we can do. How might we feel in general? Energised, in control, positive, motivated, resilient?

Me:
Okay, I've got that image in my mind.

Elain and Sharon:
Okay, let's imagine another scenario. We have an unhealthy body; this could be anything from constantly catching colds and viruses to dealing with serious illness such as heart conditions or diabetes. It could be arthritis or another condition affecting our joints or muscles. Whatever reason for our unhealthy body, we may be affected in any number of ways. If we're in pain, we might not be sleeping well and therefore we'd be experiencing tiredness and an inability to focus. If our unhealthy body stops us from firing on all cylinders we may experience low energy levels and a lack of motivation and general

oomph! If our unhealthy body affects our ability to work, we may experience financial difficulties. Our relationships may suffer. And we could go on. So how might we feel? Grumpy, irritable, low mood, depressed, loss of freedom of choice, therefore out of control?

Although both of these statements are perhaps a little sweeping, the link between our physical and mental health is undeniable. We may not always be aware of how being unhealthy affects our mind because generally it creeps up on us slowly but it clearly does.

Me:
I can be a little sedentary at times, although I do walk my dog for an hour a day. How important is exercise to resilience?

Elain and Sharon:
Those who exercise regularly are more likely to experience good health. When we exercise and our heart pumps more blood around our body, more of the neurotransmitter hormones serotonin and endorphins are released into the brain. Endorphins act as an analgesic, thereby lowering the perception of pain whilst serotonin serves to balance mood. The result is a general sense of wellbeing and energy and, of course, a stronger, healthier heart and body.

Our brain also receives increased oxygen flow when we exercise, which again allows it to perform at its best as well as to regenerate. Research shows that our brains have the capacity to adapt and change when we stimulate them through activities that push us out of our comfort zone, when we socialise and interact with others and when we learn new skills and challenge our thought patterns. Furthermore, exercise and a strong body have been linked to reduced risks of dementia, depression and anxiety.

Have you ever been for a run or other exercise and found that you are much more likely to eat healthily afterwards? That's because we become what we think. That is, when we adopt healthy behaviours, we act in a way that supports the view that we are healthy. The neurotransmitters in our brains need to be 'exercised' just like our muscles in order to make permanent changes to the way that we think. But over time, just as our muscles grow strong, if we continue to think positively about a healthy lifestyle, our thought patterns naturally support this view and so do our behaviours. So, as Henry Ford said, 'If you think you can or you think you can't, you're probably right.' The way that our minds can impact on our behaviours, which in turn influences the degree to which we are healthy or otherwise, is astonishing. In fact, scientists talk about our 'little brain' in our stomach, which holds 100 million neurotransmitters that each communicate with those in our brain in order to transfer information about our emotions. This may be experienced as our 'gut reaction' but can be a powerful way of tuning into what is right for us.

The way we think affects our behaviours, healthy or otherwise. Our chosen health-supporting or damaging behaviours reinforce a positive mind through the release of feel–good hormones, which support our self-esteem and general mental health. The body and mind are inextricably interlinked and, when we use that link, they really will support us to be our best self, physically, mentally and emotionally.

What should school leaders be doing to model wellbeing in their schools?

School leadership is always busy, demanding and often fraught, so I asked Sharon and Elain for some simple, practical advice for school leaders to help them take care of themselves, in order that they can then help others. Here are their top ten tips:

Top 10 wellbeing tips for school leaders

1 **Eat the frog first!** – As Brian Tracy advocates (p. 89), each morning, or at the end of the day before, prepare a short 'sub-list' from your 'to do list' of the top three things you need to achieve today (or for tomorrow). Tackle the one that inspires you the least first and set a time for it to be completed, e.g. one hour or whatever. *Try* to avoid being distracted by any other task until it's done! Then move onto the other things on your sub-list. It will help you feel more productive and motivated and achieve more in each day.

2 **Drink two to three litres of water a day** – Try having a jug or two litre bottles of water on your desk and sip at them throughout the day. Don't forget to take some in the car when you're on the move. Your bladder will get used to it and you will stop needing the loo constantly – stick with it! Expect increased energy, better skin and decreased hunger.

3 **Ditch the coffee** – Have a glass of 100 per cent fresh juice and take some deep breaths from the abdomen instead. Limit to once a day as it's high in sugar, and eat a small handful of nuts with it (unless you are a nut-free school of course), as this slows down the release of sugar, therefore keeping you energised for longer. Alternatively, eating

blueberries or bananas helps to give a slow release of energy through the day. Experiment with other non-caffeine hot drinks like fruit tea or hot water with a squeeze of lemon.

4 **Get moving** – Follow some of these simple ideas:

- If you are spending a lot of time at your desk, stand up every hour and rotate and flex your shoulders and your feet at the ankle.
- Take every opportunity to walk – walk to a colleague to ask them a question; walk for at least ten minutes at lunchtime, even if it is just around the school grounds. Take an umbrella and warm coat. The weather should not be a barrier – in fact, it's very liberating walking in the rain!
- Get your heart rate up (to the point you can't hold a normal conversation) at least two or three times a week. Try new things – run, swim, join a class, gym or sports club. Get something going at work. (Talk to us at WELLBEING4LIFE about a work boot camp INSET. We'll come to you with all the kit – convenient and a great team-booster!)

5 **Ground two to three times a day** – Or whenever needed. Whether standing or seated, place both feet flat on the floor and feel the ground beneath them. Breath in for four seconds, hold for seven seconds, breathe out for eight seconds. Repeat two or three times. Close your eyes if possible (not when driving, obviously!). Make this part of your daily routine and you should feel calmer and more in control of your stress levels.

6 **Connect** – When you can, use the phone or walk to speak to somebody instead of emailing. You'll probably get the answer quicker and be able to tick jobs off, and you'll also feel more cheerful and positive too! People will also appreciate the personal touch.

7 **Eat lunch away from your desk** – Lunchtime meetings are a way of life in many schools, but ensure you do get a short break and eat away from your desk, office or classroom, ideally outside (weather permitting!).

8 **Eat fresh and clean** – Try some of these ideas:

- Avoid processed food. If it's got a long list of ingredients or it's not in its natural form, it's not good for you. Don't eat it!

- Ditch the sugar – feel more energised. Snack on a small handful of nuts (six to eight) or, if you are a nut-free school, berries instead. Both will give a slow release of energy.
- Eat breakfast, lunch, dinner and two snacks every day.
- Be prepared – plan and bring food to work such as berries, natural full-fat yogurt (low-fat is sugar-loaded), oatcakes, hummus or cottage cheese.

9 **Limit alcohol** – To zero to one glass per work evening and feel more energised, alert and slimmer! When you do drink, have one glass of water for every alcoholic drink.

10 **Practise good sleep hygiene** – Get at least eight hours a night on a work night. Have a technology detox from at least one hour before bed. No emails, phones, tablets – nothing! Use the time to talk and actively listen. Be present and hear what people are saying. Make it a household ban.

Sharon de Caestecker and Elain Crewe

Courtesy of WELLBEING4LIFE

Many of you reading this may have also gone into leadership roles in your twenties. You need to pay the rent or, if you are lucky enough to have got onto the property ladder, your mortgage. The retirement age is going up, so many of you are going to be in leadership roles for the long haul, eclipsing my 23 years even. That is perfectly 'doable' but only if you make self-care a priority.

Ladies and gentlemen, put simply, you need a plan!

You don't necessarily have to make huge alterations to your way of life; sometimes a series of smaller changes may be all that is needed.

Time to reflect

Consider carefully the list below. Which do you think you could commit to in order to make a difference to your working day? Make notes about what you will change.

- Where possible, eat the frog first each day.

- Drink two to three litres of water a day.
- Ditch (or at least reduce) the coffee.
- Get moving. Find opportunities to move around the school at break times and lunchtimes.
- Ground two or three times a day.
- Connect with other adults. Where possible, go and see people instead of emailing them.
- Eat lunch away from your desk.
- Eat fresh and clean.
- Limit your alcohol intake.
- Practise good sleep hygiene and turn off devices one hour before bed.

Now to fully commit to this plan (which, let's face it, is the harder part – what, really no burgers?), show your plan to someone at work and someone at home so they know what you are trying to achieve and can suitably admonish you if you go astray!

How can school leaders promote wellbeing amongst staff?

There are lots of ways in which you as a school leader can model wellbeing, but let's start with the key three:

1. Recognise that wellbeing is part of your role.
2. Ensure wellbeing is embedded in your values.
3. Lead by example.

1. Recognise that wellbeing is part of your role

School leaders are in a unique position with the ability to either negatively or positively influence wellbeing across the school. At this stage, a definition of wellbeing may be of value:

The National Institute for Health and Care Excellence (NICE, 2017) defines wellbeing as:

> *The subjective state of being healthy, happy, contented, comfortable and satisfied with one's quality of life. Mental wellbeing relates to a person's emotional and psychological wellbeing. This includes self-esteem and the ability to socialise and cope in the face of adversity.*

Perhaps you think this definition is too broad in relation to the workplace setting; perhaps as a school leader you see it as beyond the scope of your remit?

However, this definition highlights that it's impossible to distinguish between the individual at home and the individual at work. People's work and domestic lives have become entwined, so we cannot afford to make a distinction between the two. Professor Dame Carol Black published her groundbreaking review of the health of Britain's working age population in 2008, and in it she states that the workplace plays a key role in promoting the nation's health and wellbeing. The review also advocated a new, joined-up approach to health and wellbeing at work and beyond, highlighting the wider impacts upon society.

A lack of personal and/or workplace wellbeing leads to a ripple effect in terms of staff morale, productivity, team cohesion, effectiveness and the sense of energy and vitality, which is the lifeblood of any organisation. Put simply, these issues are very much a part of your role as a school leader, thereby placing wellbeing as an integral part of your remit.

2. Ensure wellbeing is embedded in your values

There is no one workplace wellbeing formula that can be applied across all organisations. Instead it has to be aligned with the values and culture of individual settings. So, let me ask you a question – do you know what your organisation's values are? This brings us back to the first balloon discussed in Chapter 1 of this book (p. 9) – a sense of purpose. Are those values apparent to all in the workplace? Are they apparent to visitors to the organisation? In other words, are those values actually put into practice? For example, there might be a value of open communication put into practice with an open-door policy, but is it really an open door or is it just slightly ajar?

So why are we talking about values in relation to workplace wellbeing? Values are what we stand for; they represent our unique individual essence, guiding our behaviour and informing our personal code of conduct – of course the same can be said personally and organisationally. Values are important because when we honour our values we reach fulfilment. When we don't honour our values we adopt bad habits that fail to serve us, creating conflict, stress and emotional and physical distress. Values are who we are and also reflect who the organisation is. We tend to get a physical sense when we live out of alignment with our values, a sort of gut instinct that for many can be felt in our chest or in the pit of our stomach. As a school leader, you are encouraged to become clear on what your organisational values are, so you can communicate them verbally and behaviourally and align any wellbeing initiative with them in order to engage others and to develop a meaningful wellbeing strategy, which is a world apart from the commonly adopted tick-box approach.

Think back to the question we raised earlier about how visible your organisational values are (p. 151). The value of open communication in the context of workplace wellbeing may now be quite different. Open communication from this perspective may see members of staff who feel able to talk about anything, including those issues that can often be seen as taboo, such as stress or being overwhelmed, in order that it can be dealt with appropriately and early before it really takes a hold.

Organisational values should underpin policies and procedures, with wellbeing initiatives threaded through all policies instead of a stand-alone policy in isolation. Your commitment to staff wellbeing should be clearly translated into policy, and the staff handbook is a great place to start.

3. Lead by example

The new science of happiness has led to the study of how people experience their lives, which also takes into account what they were doing, who they were with and how they felt; the disturbing news is that the time of day that was most disliked is the time they spend with their boss! If you are in a position of leadership, this is pretty scary stuff, suggesting that leaders are not currently doing such a great job in terms of promoting staff satisfaction and wellbeing.

Workplace wellbeing has to be led from the top and the first step is to review your own wellbeing. Take another look at the NICE definition of wellbeing (p. 151). How healthy, happy, contented, comfortable and satisfied do you feel? How would you rate your self-esteem and your ability to cope in the face of adversity? How productive do you feel and how would you describe your relationships with others? Have you taken some time to consider what your own values are and whether you are living in alignment with them?

Starting with your self is a great place to start. Don't just 'talk the talk' but actually 'walk the walk'. Setting off on the walk can feel daunting and you may be wondering where to start. To avoid being overwhelmed, just choose three things that you could do differently. Perhaps you can start by looking at our top ten wellbeing tips (p. 147) and choose three of them to experiment with. It's a good idea to keep a record of your experimentations, noting how your actions make you feel and the impact they have on your productivity, creativity, sleep, etc. Remember, we are all different and what works for one may not work for another, so the experimentation element is key.

Think about the culture of the organisation – does it support wellbeing? For example, do members of staff generally take a lunch break away from their desk? It's suggested that the way employees spend their lunch break is a good indicator of the social aspect of an organisation's culture and how staff feel about their workload. Often, employees who feel overwhelmed will eat lunch at their desk to make the most of every minute. One of the biggest contributors to depression, stress and anxiety is a sense of work overload. Conversely, if employees eat together or spend their lunch break going on walks or other non-work-related activities, it's a good sign that the culture makes people feel they can use that time for themselves. Eating with colleagues increases workplace satisfaction. The benefits of socialising are similar to those of exercise in that stress and blood pressure levels are reduced and you generally feel happier than you did before. Additionally, those who socialise are more productive. Getting away from the desk and engaging in some form of physical movement and new visual stimulation gives the brain a chance to reboot, meaning that employees return to the desk with a fresher perspective.

So, the question is, what does the culture of your school say to staff about taking a break? Is it frowned upon? Is it actively encouraged? What do you do? Are you leading by example?

Of course, leadership can be a lonely place, so how about getting some like-minded colleagues on board? Perhaps a group of wellbeing champions could be developed across the school or maybe some light-hearted inter-departmental wellbeing challenges could be devised – which department can walk the most steps challenge, anybody?

Food for thought, folks.

Of course, you are going to be little good to anyone if you are not in a good place yourself. It is rather like the oxygen mask scenario.

The oxygen mask scenario

You are told in the preflight safety briefing on aeroplanes (I know this because, as I've said before, I always pay very close attention!) that in the event of the cabin depressurising, oxygen masks will descend from the panel above and that you should pull them to get the oxygen flowing and place over your face using the attached elastic band. So far, so good, but then they tell you that if you are travelling with children, you should attend to your own mask before trying to help them. What? It goes against every instinct as a parent, but the logic is clear. If you fall unconscious yourself, then you are in no position to help anyone else.

The analogy is clear. You don't need me to spell it out.

Summary

- School leaders tend to be selfless individuals for whom self-care is often not a priority.
- Many leaders tend to see investing in their own wellbeing as selfish when actually the truth is to the contrary.
- Not investing in your own wellbeing can ultimately be detrimental to your own welfare as well as that of colleagues and pupils.
- There is a clear link between mental and physical health.
- The link between the wellbeing of the individual at home and at work is indistinguishable.
- Concentrating on the wellbeing of both our body and mind helps us to be our best, physically, mentally and emotionally.
- School leaders are in a unique position to positively (or negatively) influence wellbeing in their schools.
- Wellbeing needs to be central to the values of any school.
- Recognise that wellbeing is part of your role.
- School leaders need to 'walk the walk' as well as 'talk the talk', starting with their own wellbeing. Lead by example.

10 Turning adversity into opportunity

Something very beautiful happens to people when their world has fallen apart: a humility, a nobility, a higher intelligence emerges at just the point when our knees hit the floor.

Marianne Williamson

Our trip is almost at an end and so we move to our final balloon – our final trait of resilience – leadership: the ability to turn adversity into opportunity. I want to take you back to the weekend of Saturday 5 December 2015. Storm Desmond was battering the western coast of the UK. Amongst the worst affected areas was Cumbria. A new record for the amount of rain in a 24-hour period was created over the weekend with 341.4mm recorded at Honister Pass. Rivers burst their banks, a number of bridges collapsed and by Sunday morning flood waters had reached first floor level. More than 1,000 people were evacuated from houses in parts of Cumbria and the Scottish Borders, and tens of thousands of homes were left without power.

On the Sunday morning, in the village of Crosby-on-Eden near Carlisle, Ayesha Weston, headteacher of the village primary school, came out to assess any damage. She had no idea what to expect. There was a 'lake' surrounding the school. She couldn't get near it. The water was three or four feet high in places. The school had flooded before but never to this extent. Ayesha remembers thinking to herself at the time that she might have to shut the school for a few days. She chuckles looking back, thinking that she might be able to reopen on the Wednesday.

Ayesha managed to get in on the Monday, and what she saw was absolutely heartbreaking. Crosby-on-Eden C of E Primary is a small school with four mixed-age classes. The Nursery and Reception classroom was a later addition to the school and had been built a little higher. The water had reached the level of the doorway but had thankfully not got in. They were able to use that classroom as a base but with that exception, everything else in the school was ruined.

The staff were brilliant. They came in with their wellies on and began to clear out the school, logging all the items that had to be disposed of. They filled skip after skip with furniture, resources and all the children's work, which was beyond rescue.

The hard thing was that the school had converted to be a stand-alone academy in 2012. They had no one to go to and no idea what to do in such devastating circumstances. There was no academy trust or local authority to tap into. It was all down to Ayesha and her business manager, Lydia Wood, to sort the situation out and Ayesha was only 18 months into her first headship. She says that Lydia is the unsung hero of this story, as she (Ayesha) got all the coverage as the spokesperson for the school but she would never have been able to do it without Lydia.

Mobile phone reception in the area is not good and the internet server was down, so Ayesha had to use her car as a mobile office and park it in the one place on the playground where she could get a reasonable signal, working in the freezing cold. Having managed to make contact with the loss adjuster, he came out on the Tuesday. He was extremely helpful and supportive, guiding Ayesha and Lydia through the process and what needed to be done in what order.

They brought in people to professionally strip the school. It was gutted – the plaster was removed from walls, leaving exposed brickwork; it was a shell of a school. The phone calls and emails from Ayesha's makeshift office in the car never stopped. The two of them were sorting things out until 10.00pm on Christmas Eve before giving themselves Christmas Day off. It was all-consuming. The focus was always on the children; that was their sense of purpose, many of whom had also been flooded out at home. 'We have to get this right for the children,' Ayesha and Lydia would remind themselves, and it was that thought that kept them going.

The children had lost two weeks of their education at the end of the term and Christmas is a big thing in primary schools, with plays and parties. The school was decimated but they were adamant that Christmas must still happen. It was through the goodwill of the local community that the children didn't miss out. The local secondary school offered the use of their hall so that the plays could go ahead. The children were fantastic and not at all fazed by the size of the stage they were standing on. A school governor offered her soft play and farm park business as a venue for the children's parties. They even managed to get the kids to the local panto as planned. It was just what the school and, indeed, the whole community needed.

The biggest priority was to get the children back in school as close as possible to the start of term in January, which they did manage within four days of the official start of term. Four Portakabins™ were brought onto site as the work continued in the main building, a much more complicated operation than you might expect. Buying in some basic stock, staff sold it to the children that they were going on a great adventure for the next six months! The more you tell other people something, the more you start to believe it yourself and the enthusiasm was infectious. Governors and parents came to see this as an adventure too: an opportunity to be seized.

Ayesha believes that none of the children lost anything (other than their work) as a result of the flood and would not look back on their six months in the Portakabins™ as a bad experience, because the staff carried on as they always had, trying to make things as much fun as possible, making new resources and creating beautiful displays. Despite the logistical issues such as staggered break times and lunchtimes the whole staff made it work.

A devastating natural event ultimately strengthened, rather than weakened, the school. It brought staff together and indeed brought the whole community much closer. On a practical level, the children and staff got a bright and modern interior (which the children helped to design) to what had previously been a somewhat dark and dilapidated building. The building is as vibrant now as the children who are in it.

On a personal note, Ayesha discovered an inner resilience that she did not know she had, but found it in her relentless focus to make things right for the children and the ability to pull people together and lead them through a time of crisis.

Despite the heartache and the tireless efforts of all involved, Ayesha has said that if she could go back in time and prevent it from happening, she does not think she would. They have a beautiful environment for their children to learn in, much stronger relationships with parents and a stronger connection with the community they serve.

Ayesha was presented an award, and rightly so, at the Cumbria Primary and Secondary Heads Conference in 2016. She accepted it, on behalf of the school.

> *You will never know yourself or the strength of your relationships until both have been tested by adversity.*
>
> J. K. Rowling (2008)

Most people entering into school leadership do so in the hope, if not the absolute confidence, that it will go well – that they will come out the other side relatively unscathed and that someone will stand up at their retirement party and raise a glass and a toast saying '(S)he really made a difference.' Whilst this last point may well be the truth, the chances of coming through a long career in leadership unscathed are relatively small. Into every leader's life a little rain must fall – so bring an umbrella.

Realistically, no one will have a 100 per cent success rate, and how we handle times of difficulty are the moments that define our character and subsequently our leadership style.

Thankfully, situations of devastation such as befell Crosby-on-Eden school are rare, but other crises such as the death of a pupil or a member of staff are not uncommon. Mercifully, this was one particular bullet that I did manage to dodge in a 23-year leadership career. I can only begin to imagine the impact that such an event must have both on a school and its wider community and would not presume to offer advice here. You are best off contacting your educational psychologist for that.

Smaller-scale crises are bound to befall a school from time to time – anything from a broken boiler to an unexpected dump of snow. In such circumstances, I believe that I led from the front! The second school where I was head comprised 27 classrooms, six playgrounds and two entrances. We were blessed with a fantastic site manager, Maurice, and an equally wonderful caretaker, Chris, who would always go above and beyond the call of duty. But getting paths cleared of snow to allow safe entrance into the school in time for the children to arrive (and thus stay open) was a tall order, so I would always get out there and shovel snow with them. But I was not the only one. I had some fantastic members of staff and on such occasions job descriptions would go out of the window, people would roll up their sleeves (well, metaphorically anyway; it would be freezing cold after all!) and do whatever needed to be done to keep the kids safe and warm.

Slightly further afield, but still snow-related, Ross Morrison McGill recently related to me the story of a school ski trip, which he helped to lead.

> *Once, we went on a ski trip and the coach broke down. We had to sleep in the coach in freezing conditions. We were parked outside a petrol station in the French Alps. Staff members were on patrol all through the night but they worked together in a situation of genuine adversity. With a bit of begging, the petrol station owner opened up and supplied the kids and staff with hot coffee and croissants to keep people warm in the freezing temperatures. Staff were negotiating with coach companies, trying to arrange alternative transport and assisting mechanics when they arrived.*
>
> Ross Morrison McGill

It has been my experience too, over the years, that times of crisis in schools bring out the best in people, because ultimately, *they* want what is best for the children. However, they will need decisive leadership in order for their efforts to be effective.

> *In situations of adversity, leaders need to keep that cool, calm head, step back a little from the immediate and start to delegate and give people's willing efforts direction.*
>
> Ross Morrison McGill

Time to reflect

Have you ever experienced a crisis in school brought on by *external* forces?

- What happened?
- What were your feelings as the crisis broke?
- How did you act?
- Is there anything that you would do differently faced with the same situation again?
- What learning did you take from this as a school?

Dealing with challenges and adversity

Admittedly some challenges we face can be completely unpredictable. For example, I remember an occasion when the A50, which ran past our school, was closed before school in both directions due to a major accident. A significant number of members of staff were stuck in stationary traffic and many of our fabulous teaching assistants volunteered to be deployed to take classes until their teachers could make it in. It could not have been predicted or planned for but it needed coordination to make sure all 27 classes had an adult in front of them.

However, other challenges we face may be unpredictable in their timing, but we know that they are coming. The prime example of this is an Ofsted or Estyn inspection. You might not know *when* they are coming but you know one day they will! By plotting out your initial actions and making clear the roles of other people, you (and they) will feel calmer, more in control of the situation and less stressed. This in turn will help you maintain a clear head and make considered decisions.

As a highly experienced interim head and a leader who has been through over 20 Ofsted inspections, Patrick Ottley-O'Connor has a clear plan so that the senior leadership team (SLT) and admin team know exactly what to do 'when an inspector calls'. What follows is Patrick's crib sheet for just such an occasion, which he has kindly given me permission to reproduce here. Whilst this is clearly set out in the context of a large secondary school, the format can easily be adapted to almost any school situation to ensure a calm and orderly response once that call comes.

The initial phone call

The phone call notifying the school of a section 8 inspection will usually take place between midday and 2pm on the day before the inspection.

If the school cannot be contacted, the inspection team may arrive unannounced. If the headteacher is unavailable, Ofsted will ask to speak to the most senior member of staff available.

Therefore: staff in reception are briefed to put *all* Ofsted calls immediately through to my PA. The PA is briefed for three scenarios:

1. I'm in the building

- Find and alert me.
- Once informed, give me 60 seconds to compose myself at my desk before putting the call through.
- Contact the deputies to join me during the call ASAP.
- Bring me a coffee!

- Alert the Chair of Governors (and the Chief Executive Office of the Multi-Academy Trust (MAT CEO) if applicable) that the call is being taken and that I'll phone them later.
- PA to take notes during the call as an 'insurance' note-taker.

2. I'm not in the building

- Alert me by mobile.
- Once informed, give me 60 seconds to compose myself at my desk before putting the call through to my mobile.
- Inform the deputies and let them know that I want them in an office to await my call.
- Alert the Chair of Governors (and MAT CEO) that the call is being taken off-site and that I'll phone them later.

3. I'm not in the building and cannot be reached by phone

- Find and alert the deputies.
- Once informed, give them 60 seconds to compose themself/themselves at a desk before putting the call through (they should open this pro forma).
- Bring them a drink of their choice… lay off the hard stuff!
- Alert the Chair of Governors (and MAT CEO) that the call is being taken by the deputy/deputies as I have not been contacted yet and that they will be phoned later.
- PA to take notes during the call as an 'insurance' note-taker.

Reproduced by kind permission of Patrick Ottley-O'Connor

Taking this template, how could your school adapt this, so that key members of staff all know what to do in the opening moments of the process?

We have assumed so far that the crisis the school might be experiencing is caused by an outside influence such as an act of nature, mechanical failure or a visit from your friendly neighbourhood inspection team. However, in reality, crises can be caused from within; a supply teacher not following the school's behaviour policy or an unfortunate remark made by a flustered teacher at parents' evening can be enough to spark a complaint, which if not satisfactorily resolved can have the potential to escalate to something out of all proportion to the original issue, causing a lot of stress to all parties involved. These are my two golden rules:

1. **Don't try to defend the indefensible** – It is a natural instinct to try to back your staff up of course, and rightly so, but defending actions or words that you know to be wrong does them no favours in the long run, as it is only likely to protract any complaint and ongoing complaints can be very stressful (believe me, I know!). It also potentially damages your credibility with parents and the reputation of the school when it becomes the hot topic of discussion with the 'school gate committee'.
2. **The word 'sorry' goes a long way** – I always tried to include the word 'sorry' somewhere in a face-to-face conversation with parents or even in responding to letters of complaint. People do like to hear you use that word. Saying 'sorry' does not necessarily mean that you accept their viewpoint, or that the school, or the individual member of staff in question, were necessarily in the wrong. Often, 'I can see you are very upset about this and I am truly sorry you felt that you needed to come in' will suffice. You are acknowledging and accepting their viewpoint without actually accepting any liability. 'Sorry' has diffused many a situation in my career!

As a school leader, you are also capable of creating your own crisis!

In my first term of headship, I received a letter of complaint from the father of Andrew to say that his son was being bullied by another boy – let's call him Alex, because that was his name (no, only kidding, I generally change names to protect the innocent, or the guilty, as the case may be). It was 20 years ago and I cannot remember the specifics, but I do recall that it was fairly low-level playground name-calling. It had, nonetheless, really upset Andrew and was clearly not acceptable. I spoke to Alex, who seemed genuinely remorseful and made him apologise to Andrew face to face. The two boys went off quite happily and I rang Andrew's dad to explain what I had done. He seemed reasonably happy. Job well done, James!

Fast forward to the end of the academic year, and I came across the letter of complaint amongst a pile of papers. (A tidy desk was never really my thing, as anyone who has worked with me will tell you.) I reread the letter, and as nothing more had come of it, and being rather naïve and over-confident in my abilities, I shredded the letter.

Forward again ten months, and the issue raised its ugly head again and Andrew's father wrote me a second letter that referenced some of the details of the first, which, of course, I no longer had. Not being blessed with the best of memories, even at that time, I had to confess to Dad in a face-to-face meeting with him that I could not recall much of the first incident. Put it this way, the meeting did not go well – to put it mildly – but it probably did me a favour in the long run, because I learned from my mistake, and kept all letters of complaint from that point on.

Forward once more 15 years and a child in my second headship had a tooth knocked out by another pupil who was swinging round one of those plant pot stilts on a rope that are popular lunchtime playground equipment. After an initial flurry of correspondence, things had quietened down until two years later when the parents tried to sue the school. Fortunately, I had all the paperwork!

My experience with Andrew's father was painful and more than a little humiliating. As leaders, none of us set out to, or want to, make mistakes, but *we will* make mistakes nonetheless.

Across 23 years as a school leader, I learned more from my mistakes than I ever did my successes.

There is nothing worse than going through a difficult time in your professional or personal life and feeling as though all the heartbreak and anguish was for nothing. Adversity can, if we let it, make us feel drained and defeated. We will often feel like retreating into a corner and licking our wounds out of sight like a wounded animal but, somewhere inside, a part of us wants to make sense of the experience. We want to make them count for something positive, where the pain we have endured was not for nothing. My first book was about just that – trying to make sense of my experiences, and seeking to help others avoid some of the mistakes that I had made in my career. If I could do that, even for a handful of people, the painful times (and there were far more good times than bad) would have meaning.

> *That which does not kill us makes us stronger.*
>
> Friedrich Nietzsche

Time to reflect

Have you ever experienced a crisis in school brought on by *internal* forces?

- What happened?
- What were your feelings as the crisis broke?
- How did you act?
- Is there anything that you would do differently faced with the same situation again?

- What learning did you take from this as a school?

How can we begin to turn the inevitable adversities into advantage?

There are some simple steps you can take. None are rocket science, but in your busy working week, they are worth a reminder:

Top tips for turning adversities into advantage

1. **Avoid slipping into a state of denial** – You are where you are. A state of denial is likely to delay you in addressing the issue and getting yourself out of the situation. Acknowledge the reality of the situation but do not dwell and brood on what has happened. Try to see change as a challenge and an opportunity to learn rather than fall into despair. Acknowledging the reality of the situation does not necessarily mean that you have to agree with the verdict, but it is in acknowledging it that we are able to move on.
2. **Depersonalise the issue** – Not easy I know, but the more you take your situation personally, the harder it is to be objective and look for ways forward.
3. **Gain outside perspective** – Talk to people whom you trust both personally and professionally and gain their objective perspective. The more emotionally involved you are in a situation, the harder it is to maintain a proper perspective.
4. **Remember, nothing lasts forever and neither will your current problems** – Our difficulties do have an expiry date. We may not be able to predict when it will be over, but please do know that it will eventually come to an end. Ian Gilbert compares this to a giant fallen tree. You may not see a way around it or over it, but there usually is a way. Even if

there is not, the fallen tree itself will not last forever. It breaks down and rots away over time (Gilbert, 2004). There are a handful of parents who made vexatious complaints some years back, whose names I struggle to remember now (and I never would have believed that that would have happened). The sun will come out again, sooner or later. Remember that.

5. **The next thing you need to do is broaden the context of your situation** – As leadership experts James Kouzes and Barry Posner suggest, staff will be looking to you for a steer (Kouzes and Posner, 2014). Your situation is unlikely to be unique. You have to convince people that they can get through the challenges you are facing much as other schools have done before you. What is the bigger picture here? How can you help staff to see that other schools have come through similar difficulties?
6. **Act quickly to mobilise your staff and your resources** – Believe in yourself and your ability to turn this situation around to your advantage. If you don't believe in yourself, no one else is likely to. They need to believe that you can, and will, lead them through this.
7. **Ask yourself, what is another way of looking at this situation?** – What might be the silver lining in all of this? Keep your staff focused on what is possible. Strive to keep the children at the centre of everything that you do. Keep your focus on the things that really matter. You need to act positively and assertively.

   Taking charge of change is how you invent your future, rather than just letting it happen to you.

   Kouzes and Posner (2014)

8. **Do not be afraid to show your human side in times of adversity** – Staff need to know that you are in it with them and that you too are taking your share of any hardship. Failure to do so will invite cynicism and resentment and make the process of moving forward more difficult.
9. **Staff members need to know that you have confidence in them and in their abilities to make necessary changes** – It is difficult to do that if you are not visible. Maintain a presence and communicate regularly; show them you care.
10. **Remember, adversity can be the greatest teacher** – The more you are able to see the benefit that results from it, the more good you will find in it and the more positive you will feel.

Summary

- School leaders can find themselves in times of challenge and adversity for a whole host of reasons, including, sometimes, their own actions.
- A crisis often brings out the best in staff, but willing efforts need strategic and level-headed direction from school leaders.
- Prepare, as far as possible, plans for predictable situations, e.g. inspections.
- Mistakes are part and parcel of school leadership. Try to look on them as learning experiences.
- Avoid denial and acknowledge your situation, if not the verdict.
- Depersonalise your situation.
- Gain an outside perspective on events from someone you trust.
- Nothing lasts forever and neither will your difficulties.
- Broaden your context and look at the broader picture.
- Act quickly to mobilise your staff and your resources.
- Find the silver lining.
- Take your share of any hardship.
- Show staff that you have confidence in them.
- Remember, adversity can be the greatest teacher. Learn what you can from it.

Conclusion

The thing that is really hard, and really amazing, is giving up on being perfect and beginning the work of becoming yourself.

Anna Quindlen (2004)

As with all things, we have come to an end.

School leaders are some of the most incredible people on this planet. They are determined to make a difference. As we come to the end of this book together, I want to thank you. You do a remarkable and hugely important job, often in challenging circumstances. The balloons – traits – of resilience that we have shared are not exclusive and we all possess them in some measure.

Leadership is a challenging but rewarding game, and I hope that has come over in this book. I am often asked whether, if I was given my time again, I would go into a school leadership role and my answer is always the same. Yes! For the most part, I loved it. As I said in Chapter 7 (p. 115), I had, roughly six bad terms out of 70 – that's pretty good going, I think! Yes, there are many things I would do differently; I would certainly be a little kinder to myself. It is alright not to feel okay all the time. You will, at times, feel like you are the only person feeling that way, but believe me you are not.

Rereading Andy's kind foreword, he suggests that this book is for my 25-year-old self and he is probably right! I do not approach my writing as someone who was a superhero who got everything right, but rather that experience was the biggest teacher of all.

In the fraught life that is the twenty-first-century school, we often underestimate the impact we have as a school leader; we can feel like a very small cog in a very big machine.

Let me leave you with one last thought then:

Once, there was an old man who used to go to the ocean to do his daily writing. He had a ritual of walking on the beach every morning before he began to write. Early one day, he was walking along the shore after a huge storm had passed and he found the beach covered with starfish as far as the eye could see.

In the far distance, the old man noticed a little boy approaching. As he walked, the boy paused every now and then and as he grew closer, the man could see that he kept bending down to pick something up and throw it into the sea. As the man grew closer to the boy he called out to him, saying, 'Good morning! May I ask what you are doing?'

The boy stopped in his tracks, looked up, and called back, 'Throwing starfish into the sea. The high tide has washed them up onto the beach and they will not be able to return by themselves. They will die if I leave them.'

The man came closer still and said to the boy, 'There are simply thousands of starfish on this beach. I am afraid you won't really be able to make that much of a difference.'

The boy smiled, picked up another starfish and threw it as far as he could into the sea. He turned, grinning, and said, 'Well, I've made a difference to that one!'

(Adapted from 'The Star Thrower' by Loren Eiseley, 1969)

You make a difference. Never forget that! You possess the ten traits of a successful school leader but we all need to give those balloons a little boost of inflation from time to time. I hope that I have provided you with some strategies to help.
Safe travels, my friend!

James

Bibliography

Archer, S. (2016), 'I'm the boss – 10 tips to become a great leader', *The Guardian*, www.theguardian.com/careers/2016/aug/24/boss-10-tips-to-become-great-leader-management

Bamia, C., Trichopoulou, A., Trichopoulos, D. (2008), 'Age at retirement and mortality in a general population sample: the Greek EPIC study', *American Journal of Epidemiology*, 167,(5), 561–9.

BBC (2010), 'Rolling a Reliant Robin', *Top Gear,* www.youtube.com/watch?v=QQh56geU0X8&t=187s

Bennett, R. T. (2016), *The Light in the Heart: Inspirational Thoughts for Living Your Best Life.* Self-published.

Bennis, W. (1999), 'The leadership advantage'. *Leader to Leader*, 12, 18–23.

Bergland, C. (2012), 'Building bulletproof courage: 3 simple ways to turn fear into confidence.' *Psychology Today*, www.psychologytoday.com/blog/the-athletes-way/201201/building-bulletproof-courage

Black, C. (2008), 'Working for a healthier tomorrow', London: The Stationery Office, Crown Copyright, www.gov.uk/government/publications/working-for-a-healthier-tomorrow-work-and-health-in-britain

Bligh, M. C. (2017), 'Leadership and trust' in Marques, J. and Dhiman, S. (eds), *Leadership Today: Practices for Personal and Professional Performance*. Switzerland: Springer, pp. 21–42.

Bremner, Dr J. D. with Reed, L. (2014), *You Can't Just Snap Out Of It: The Real Path to Recovery From Psychological Trauma: Introducing the START NOW Program.* USA: Laughing Cow Books.

Buck, A. (2016), *Leadership Matters: How Leaders at all Levels can Create Great Schools.* Woodbridge: John Catt Educational Ltd.

Buettner, D. (2009), 'How to live to be 100+', *TEDx Talk*, www.ted.com/talks/dan_buettner_how_to_live_to_be_100.html

Buettner, D. (2012), *The Blue Zones: 9 Lessons for Living Longer from the People Who've Lived the Longest* (2nd edn). Washington: National Geographic Publications.

Cope, A. and Whittaker, A. (2012), *The Art of Being Brilliant*. Chichester: Capstone.

Covey, S. R. (2004a), *The 7 Habits of Highly Effective People: Powerful Lessons in Personal Change* (revised edn). London: Simon & Schuster.

Covey, S. R. (2004b), *The 8th Habit: From Effectiveness to Greatness*. London: Simon & Schuster.

Covey, S. R. (2009), 'How the best leaders build trust', *Leadership Now*, www.leadershipnow.com/pvcovey.html

Day, C. and Gu, Q. (2014), *Resilient Teachers, Resilient Schools: Building and Sustaining Quality in Testing Times*. London: Routledge.

Dean, J. (2007), 'How to build courage through personality traits and states of mind', *PSYBLOG*, www.spring.org.uk/2007/08/how-to-build-courage-through.php

Diener, E., Fujita, F., Tay, L. and Biswas-Diener, R. (2012), 'Purpose, mood, and pleasure in predicting satisfaction judgments'. *Social Indicators Research* 105(3), 333–341.

Dyer, W. (2010), '"If you believe it will work out, you'll see opportunities. If you believe it won't you will see obstacles." – Dr Wayne Dyer' [Facebook post], www.facebook.com/drwaynedyer/posts/149930501687383

Eggert, M. (2007), *The Perfect Interview: All You Need to Get it Right First Time* (revised edn). London: Random House.

Eiseley, L. (1969), *The Unexpected Universe*. New York: Harcourt, Brace and World.

Ellis, A. (1994), *Reason and Emotion in Psychotherapy: A Comprehensive Method of Treating Human Disturbances* (revised edn). New York, NY: Stuart Lyle.

Eyre, C. (2017), *The Elephant In The Staffroom: How to Reduce Stress and Improve Teacher Wellbeing*. Abingdon: Routledge.

Gerver, R. (2013), *Change: Learn to Love it, Learn to Lead it*. London: Penguin.

Gerver, R. (2014), *Creating Tomorrow's Schools Today* (2nd edn). London: Bloomsbury Education.

Gilbert, I. (2004), *Little Owl's Book of Thinking: An Introduction to Thinking Skills*. Carmarthen: Crown House Publishing Ltd.

Godin, S. (2010), *Linchpin: Are You Indispensable? How to drive your career and create a remarkable future*. London: Piatkus.

Grant, L. and Kinman, G. (eds) (2014), *Developing Resilience for Social Work Practice*. London: Macmillan Education.

Greitens, E. (2015), *Resilience: Hard-won Wisdom for Winning a Better Life*. New York: Houghton Mifflin Harcourt.

Griffiths, R. (2014), 'Why is purpose important in the workplace', *The Association of Business Psychology*, www.theabp.org.uk/news/why-is-purpose-important-in-the-workplace.aspx

Hackel, E. (2016), *Ingaging Leadership: 21 Steps to Elevate Your Business*. Florida: Motivational Press, Inc.

Hilton, J. (2016), *Leading from the Edge: A School Leader's Guide to Recognising and Overcoming Stress*. London: Bloomsbury Education.

Ipsos MORI (2016), 'Veracity Index 2016', www.ipsos.com/sites/default/files/migrations/en-uk/files/Assets/Docs/Polls/ipsos-mori-veracity-index-2016-charts.pdf

Johnstone, M. (2015), *The Little Book of Resilience: How to Bounce Back from Adversity and Lead a Fulfilling Life*. London: Little Brown Book Group, Hachette.

Kamen, L. P. and Seligman, M. E. (1987), 'Explanatory style and health', *Current Psychological Research & Reviews*, 6(3), 207–218.

Karia, A. (2016), *7 Things Resilient People Do Differently: And How they can Help You Succeed in Business and Life*. Self-published.

Kerr, M. (2015), *The Humor Advantage: Why Some Businesses are Laughing all the Way to the Bank*. www.thehumoradvantage.com.

Kouzes, J. and Posner, B. (2014), *Turning Adversity into Opportunity*. San Francisco: Jossey-Bass.

Kulaga, J. (2014), 'How you can build your confidence, and keep it', *Forbes*, www.forbes.com/sites/womensmedia/2014/10/07/how-you-can-build-your-confidence-and-keep-it

Maxwell, J. C. (2000), *Failing Forward: Turning Mistakes into Stepping Stones for Success*. Nashville: Thomas Nelson.

Mayo Clinic (2017), 'Positive thinking: Stop negative self-talk to reduce stress', www.mayoclinic.org/healthy-lifestyle/stress-management/in-depth/positive-thinking/art-20043950e

McGee, P. (2012), *Self-Confidence: The Remarkable Truth of Why a Small Change can Make a Difference* (2nd edn). Chichester: Capstone.

Mendez, A. (2014), *Creative Vizualization: The Best Visualization Techniques and Tips for Creative Visualization*. Self-published.

Miller, D. (2010), *48 Days to the Work You Love: Preparing for the New Normal* (revised edn). Nashville, TN: B&H Books.

Myatt, M. (2016), *High Challenge, Low Threat: Finding the Balance*. Woodbridge: John Catt Educational Ltd.

National Institute of Clinical and Healthcare Excellence (NICE) (2017), 'Healthy workplaces: improving employee mental and physical health and wellbeing', www.nice.org.uk/guidance/qs147/chapter/Quality-statement-2-Role-of-line-managers

Osincup, P. (2016), 'Leading with laughter: The power of humor in leadership', *TEDX Talks*, www.youtube.com/watch?v=yhokMZdQ7gs

Palmer, P. J. (1999), *Let Your Life Speak: Listening for the Voice of Vocation*. San Francisco: Jossey-Bass.

Parsons, P. (2009), *The Sixty Minute Father: Take an Hour to Change Your Child's Life Forever* (revised edn). London: Hodder and Stoughton.

Potworowkski, G. (2010), 'Varieties of indecisive experience: explaining the tendency to not make timely and stable decisions' (Unpublished doctoral dissertation). University of Michigan, Ann Arbor, MI.

Quindlen, A. (2004), *Being Perfect*. New York: Random House.

Reina, D. and Reina, M. (2015), *Trust and Betrayal in the Workplace: Building Effective Relationships in Your Organisation* (3rd edn). Oakland: Berrett-Koehler.

Rowling, J. K. (1997), *Harry Potter and the Philosopher's Stone*. London: Bloomsbury.

Rowling, J. K. (2008), 'Text of J.K. Rowling's speech: the fringe benefits of failure, and the importance of imagination', *The Harvard Gazette*, https://news.harvard.edu/gazette/story/2008/06/text-of-j-k-rowling-speech/

Seligman, M. E. (2018), *Learned Optimism: How to Change Your Mind and Your Life* (2nd edn). London: Nicholas Brealey Publishing.

Siebert, A. (2005), *The Resiliency Advantage Change, Thrive Under Pressure, and Bounce Back From Setbacks: Master.* San Fransisco: Berrett-Koehler.

Sinek, S. (2009), *Start With Why: How Great Leaders Inspire Everyone to Take Action.* London: Penguin.

Sonnenberg, F. (2016), 'Complacency: the enemy of success', *Frank Sonnenberg Online*, www.franksonnenbergonline.com/blog/complacency-the-enemy-of-success/

Stanley, A. (2013), 'Andy Stanley leadership podcast: listen, learn and lead', *Black Sheep Productions*, www.blacksheepproductions.com/andy-stanley-leadership-podcast-listen-learn-and-lead/

Tasler, N. (2014), *Why Quitters Win: Decide to be Excellent.* Carlsbad: Motivational Press.

Taylor, D. (2002), *The Naked Leader: The True Paths to Success are Finally Revealed.* Chichester: Capstone.

Taylor, S. (2011), *Out of the Darkness: From Turmoil to Transformation*. London: Hay House UK.

Taylor, S. (2013), 'The power of purpose: Why is a sense of purpose so essential for our well-being?' *Psychology Today*, www.psychologytoday.com/us/blog/out-the-darkness/201307/the-power-purpose

Taylor, S. and Gollwitzer, P. (1995), 'Effects of mindset on positive illusions', *Journal of Personality and Social Psychology*, 69(2), 213–226.

Tracy, B. (2004), *Eat that Frog! Get More of the Important Things Done Today!* London: Hodder and Stoughton.

Tsai, S. P., Wendt, J. K., Donnelly, R. P., de Jong, G., Ahmed, F. S. (2005), 'Age at retirement and long term survival of an industrial population: prospective cohort study', *British Medical Journal*, 331, 995.

Vanderkam, L. (2012), *What the Most Successful People Do Before Breakfast: How to Achieve More at Work and at Home*. London: Penguin.

Vanderkam, L. (2013), *What the Most Successful People Do at Work: A Short Guide to Making Over Your Career*. London: Penguin.

Verma, N. S. (2013), '5 reasons why leaders must have a good sense of humour', *Times Jobs*, http://content.timesjobs.com/5-reasons-why-leaders-must-have-a-good-sense-of-humour/articleshow/57907763.cms

Index

Note: Italicised page numbers denote figures.